AS
CriticalThinking
for OCR

Jo Lally • Mark

n.co.uk

ort

ordering

58

Heinemann
Inspiring generations

Dedication
To all my Critical Thinking students who have made this subject so enjoyable.
Mark McBride

Heinemann Educational Publishers
Halley Court, Jordan Hill, Oxford OX2 8EJ
Part of Harcourt Education

Heinemann is a registered trademark of Harcourt Education Limited

©Harcourt Education 2006

First published 2006

10 09 08 07 06
10 9 8 7 6 5 4 3 2 1

British Library Cataloguing in Publication Data is available
from the British Library on request.

10-digit ISBN: 0 435235842
13-digit ISBN: 978 0 435235 84 0

Original illustrations © Harcourt Education Limited, 2006

Printed by CPI Bath Press

Cover photo: © M.C Escher's "Symmetry Drawing" ES7 © 2005
The M.C Escher Company-Holland. All rights reserved.

Acknowledgements
The author and publisher would like to thank the following individuals and
organisations for permission to reproduce photographs: pp 6, Alamy Images/Paul
Gapper; pp 16, Alamy Images/James Royell; pp 29, Bubbles; pp 34, Alvey and
Towers; pp 45, Harcourt Education Ltd, Gareth Boden; pp 54, Getty Images,
Photodisc; pp 57, Getty Images/Photodisc; pp 82, CHI.

We would like to thank the following people for permission to reproduce
copyrighted material: pp 39, Focus Magazine; pp 41, Nick Berg; pp 85, The New
Scientist.

Tel: 01865 888058   www.heinemann.co.uk

Contents

Introduction: What does assessing and developing arguments mean?

Unit 2 of the OCR AS Level in Critical Thinking is called 'Assessing and Developing Arguments'. But, what does this mean in practice?

Assessing an argument

There are two steps to assessing an argument:

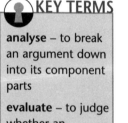

1. **Analyse** the structure of an argument, which means breaking the argument down into its component parts;
2. **Evaluate** the argument, which means judging whether it is a strong or weak argument.

Developing an argument

Developing an argument means that you will be asked to create your own argument, usually around a theme that has been suggested by the questions and passages in the exam.

Together, these skills form the basis of your assessment in the AS level exam.

There are three important skills that this unit will help you to develop and that you will be assessed on in the exam.

- The ability to **analyse** arguments
- The ability to **evaluate** arguments
- The ability to **develop** arguments.

How will this book help me to assess and develop arguments?

The nine chapters of this book will help you to build your skills so that you can tackle your exam questions, and arguments with others, with confidence. Important skills will be explained and shown at work through examples. There will be plenty of

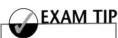

opportunities to practise the skills as you work through the book. Remember, Critical Thinking is a skill, not knowledge, so practice will really help you improve!

Chapter 1: Recognising arguments

This chapter introduces the basic parts of an argument – reasons and conclusions – and shows how they work together to make an argument persuasive. You will practise identifying the parts of an argument and how to distinguish arguments from other types of writing, such as explanations. More complicated arguments that include intermediate conclusions will also be introduced.

Chapter 2: Assumptions

Chapter 2 defines an assumption and shows how we use the term differently in critical thinking and in everyday speech. Examples show how something that is not written down may be an important part of an argument. Exercises and examples will help you write down assumptions accurately and give you some strategies for checking your exam answers.

Chapter 3: Applying the skills to longer passages

Chapter 3 helps you to extend your skills to longer arguments by showing you how to separate reasons, intermediate conclusions and the main conclusion from context, evidence and examples in a long passage. You will also practise identifying assumptions in longer passages. The chapter introduces the skills of drawing conclusions and identifying counter arguments, contradiction and inconsistency.

Chapter 4: Evaluating evidence: asking the right questions

This chapter examines how evidence can be used in an argument. It introduces questions which can help us to judge whether the use of evidence is strong or weak – is the evidence meaningful, relevant, reliable and representative? It then introduces the skill of deciding whether specific evidence would strengthen or weaken an argument.

Chapter 5: Evaluating reasons: flaws

Chapter 5 introduces patterns of reasoning which do not provide strong support for a conclusion because they are flawed. You will practise evaluating reasoning by identifying and explaining flaws in short passages. You will also practise choosing the correct explanation of a problem shown in example passages through multiple choice questions.

Chapter 6: Language, claims, reasoning

Chapter Six extends your evaluative skills. Here, you will consider problems caused by vagueness in the use of language. You will examine the status of different kinds of claims, such as fact, opinion, principles and hypothetical claims. You will also practise evaluating the ways in which principles, hypothetical reasoning and analogies make an argument stronger or weaker.

Chapter 7: Developing your own arguments

This chapter outlines the approaches and skills you will need to write short, persuasive arguments of your own. The importance of having a clear structure is introduced and explained. Examples are given to illustrate both strong and weak arguments and to help you understand what you will have to do in the exam.

Chapter 8: Preparing for the exam

This chapter will explain the general structure and content of the exam paper and give advice on how to tackle the different types of question. Worked examples will show you how to write strong answers and suggestions are given to help you prepare before the exam.

Chapter 9: Guidance to the activities

This chapter provides answers and/or sample answers for the activities in Chapters 1–7.

Recognising arguments

How do we use the word 'argument' in Critical Thinking?

An argument in Critical Thinking will always contain the following:

- a **conclusion**
- a **reason** or **reasons** to support the conclusion.

Conclusions

A conclusion is often a statement of something that we should or should not do, or something that we should believe or accept. The reason or reasons are the basis for persuading us to accept the conclusion.

Here is a very simple argument:

> *You should put on a warm coat because the weather is very cold today.*

The conclusion is: 'You should put on a warm coat.' The reason (for believing the conclusion) is: 'The weather is very cold today.'

This example also shows you that the conclusion to an argument does not have to come at the end of the text. You can put a conclusion at the end, the beginning, or indeed anywhere in the text of an argument. However, the conclusion of an argument is always at the end in terms of the meaning of the argument.

Different types of reasons

Reasons can appear in several forms in an argument. They commonly appear as statements of fact, numerical information or definitions. However they appear, they must always give support for the conclusion.

ACTIVITY ❶

Identify the reasons and conclusion in each of the following arguments:

1 The sun is very strong today and you are going to lie on the beach. You should put plenty of sun cream on.

2 Heavy snow is predicted later on. The police are advising everyone to stay at home. You should not leave home to go to work.

3 You are allergic to dog hair. The friends you are going to visit have a dog. You should take some medication to reduce your allergic reaction.

When do we use arguments?

Arguments are used when we need to persuade somebody to accept something or do something – in short, to accept our point of view.

For example, a teacher may use an argument in order to persuade students to work harder. They may put forward several reasons why working harder would be a good idea. For example, the teacher might argue like this:

> *Reason: Working harder will result in better exam grades.*
>
> *Reason: You need better grades in order to go to the university you have chosen.*
>
> *Conclusion: Therefore you should work harder.*

You will certainly have heard teachers saying something similar. The key point is to recognise an attempt to persuade somebody to do something. That makes it an argument.

The differences between arguments and other common types of language

As we have seen, the characteristic of an argument is that there is an attempt to persuade you through the use of reason – an appeal to your rational thinking processes.

However, there are other forms of language that you will come across that may appear, at first glance, to be arguments:

- **opinions** – statements of one's beliefs and ideas
- **accounts** – texts that describe events or objects
- **explanations** – attempts to give reasons why or how something is the way it is.

You need to be clear, however, that these are *not* arguments. The following sections explain why.

The difference between arguments and opinions

Many of us hold opinions and sometimes we may feel that offering our opinion to someone else will be persuasive. We may even give our opinions very strongly. However, opinions are different from arguments.

Here are some examples of opinions:

> *Taxes are too high in this country.*
>
> *Manchester United are the best football team in the world.*
>
> *Destroying the rainforest would be an environmental disaster.*

In many ways these opinions are like the conclusion to an argument. But without reasons to support them there is no argument and they are not persuasive. They demonstrate that we need to turn our opinions into arguments by supporting them with relevant reasons.

ACTIVITY ❷

Turn one of the above opinions into an argument by adding one or more relevant reasons.

The difference between arguments and accounts

Written text often seeks to describe or give an account of something, without any attempt to persuade you of anything. For example, consider this account of a summer fair:

> *Attendance at this year's summer fair was excellent. There was a range of stalls selling jam and homemade cakes and several rides to amuse the younger children present. Local MP Tom Smith described the event as a 'great success'.*

There is no attempt here to persuade anyone about the fair, and so no argument. The text gives an account of what happened.

ACTIVITY ❸

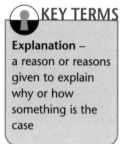

REMEMBER

Arguments need to have both a conclusion and one or more reasons supporting the conclusion.

Decide whether each of the following passages is an argument, opinion or account:

a) We had a balcony overlooking the bay, excellent food and wine and a nice room. It was a really good holiday.

b) It will be crowded in Brighton. It is a Bank Holiday and it will take us ages to get there in the traffic.

c) I will want to go on holiday after my exams. I find being by the sea very relaxing and I will certainly need a rest after all that hard work. I should book a holiday at a seaside resort.

d) It is obvious that increasing prison sentences will reduce crime.

The difference between arguments and explanations

Arguments and explanations can appear quite similar at first glance. We need to be able to spot the difference between them.

KEY TERMS

Explanation – a reason or reasons given to explain why or how something is the case

Explanations give reasons that intend to show why something is the case. There is no attempt to persuade us of something as the statement that is explained will be easily accepted. An explanation will be a statement of accepted fact with one or more other statements that explain how this came about.

For example, imagine that your Critical Thinking teacher arrives at a lesson with her ankle in plaster. There is no doubt about this and no need to persuade anyone that her ankle is in plaster. However, your curiosity may have been aroused and you might want an explanation of why her ankle is in plaster.

Your teacher might give you the following explanation:

> *My ankle is in plaster because I have torn my Achilles tendon in my ankle playing tennis. The best treatment for torn tendons is to immobilise the joint in plaster.*

ACTIVITY ④

! REMEMBER

Arguments are not just a reason or reasons that support a conclusion. They have to persuade rather than explain.

For each of the following passages, decide whether it is an argument or an explanation.

a) The train has not arrived at the station. This is because a tree has fallen and blocked the line.

b) The traffic is unusually heavy today. It is very important for you to get to school on time. You should catch an earlier bus than usual.

c) GCSE results have improved steadily over the last five years. We are seeing the effects of better teaching and improved government funding for schools.

d) A family with small children wanting a pet should get a dog rather than a cat. Cats can scratch small children when they are picked up and children will always want to pick up a cat. Dogs are too big to pick up and like children more than cats.

Exploring the structure of arguments
Reason and conclusion indicators

So far we have been looking at the basic form of an argument. Being able to identify an argument and its component parts is an important skill in Critical Thinking. However, it is not always the case that passages will have the conclusion last and the reasons first. In many arguments we may find that the conclusion comes before the reasons. So we cannot rely on the order of statements to help us judge whether an argument is present.

● KEY TERMS

Argument indicator – a word or short phrase that helps us identify the parts of an argument. For example, 'because' indicates a reason and 'therefore' indicates a conclusion

However, we are helped by the fact that arguments often contain useful words, called **argument indicators**, that 'signal' to us what part of the argument we are looking at.

Here are some examples of argument indicators:

- Words that indicate a *reason*: because, as, since, due to.
- Words that indicate a *conclusion*: therefore, thus, hence, so, it follows, should, consequently.

Look out for some of these words in the following passage:

> *We should all try and recycle more of our kitchen waste, since this would reduce the amount of waste taken to landfill sites and also because kitchen waste can be turned into useful compost.*

In this example, 'should' indicates the conclusion, and 'since' and 'because' signal the two reasons. Taken together, these words help us to identify that there is an argument present; on their own, the words help us to identify its component parts.

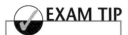

EXAM TIP

Being able to identify an argument, as well as the component parts of an argument, is a very important skill in Unit 2.

Although not all arguments contain argument indicators, we can still use them to our advantage by putting them into the argument to check that we have correctly identified its constituent parts. Here is one of the arguments in Activity 3 rewritten to include some indicator words. It may sound a bit clumsy as you read it to yourself, but the important thing is to check that it makes sense:

> ***Because** I want to go on holiday after my exams*
> ***because** I find being by the sea very relaxing*
> ***because** I will certainly need a rest after all that hard work*
> ***therefore**, I should book a holiday at a seaside resort.*

ACTIVITY ❺

! REMEMBER

Inserting the words 'because' and 'therefore' into an argument can help you check that you have correctly identified the separate parts of an argument. The text should still make sense if you have put them in the right place.

Below are three arguments that do not include argument indicators. Rewrite them with the words 'because' or 'therefore' in the correct place to help you identify the reasons and the conclusion.

a) Trains are a better way to travel than a car. It is possible to read during the journey and there is no need to worry about traffic jams or breakdowns.

b) Football is not as exciting as commentators suggest. Many games end 0–0 and results only matter for teams at the top or bottom of a table.

REMEMBER

R stands for **reason** and indicates statements that support a conclusion.

C stands for **conclusion** and identifies the statement that we should believe or accept.

Argument indicator shorthand

It is often convenient in Critical Thinking to use a 'shorthand' way of indicating the parts of an argument that show we have already checked the 'because' and 'therefore' words fit. We use 'R' to represent reasons and 'C' to represent conclusions.

When we add this shorthand, the argument on page 9 looks like this:

> R1   I want to go on holiday after my exams.
>
> R2   I find being by the sea very relaxing.
>
> R3   I will certainly need a rest after all that hard work.
>
> C   I should book a holiday at a seaside resort.

We will use this shorthand throughout the book. You may also find it a useful shorthand when you are writing your own arguments (see Chapter 7).

Simple arguments with more than one reason

As we have seen, an argument can contain several reasons that support the conclusion. There are two basic ways that reasons can be used to persuade us to accept the conclusion:

KEY TERMS

Independently supporting – when two or more reasons are given to support a conclusion and each reason on its own supports that conclusion

Jointly supporting – when two or more reasons are given to support a conclusion, but they only support that conclusion when taken together

- The reasons may act *independently*. This means that each reason, on its own, supports the conclusion.
- The reasons may act *jointly*. The reasons do not support the conclusion individually, but they do when taken together.

Look at these two examples:

> R1   Animal experiments cause a great deal of suffering.
>
> R2   The results of animal experiments are rarely applicable to humans.
>
> C   The continued use of animals in experiments cannot be justified.
>
>
> R1   Animal experiments must only be carried out if there are no alternative methods available.
>
> R2   In recent years, computer modelling techniques have become very useful as alternatives to animal experiments.
>
> C   There should be a reduction in the number of animal experiments conducted.

In the first argument, *either* reason can support the conclusion on its own. Together, they make the argument more persuasive. In the second argument, *both* reasons are needed to support the conclusion, as they only work together. (The first reason suggests that animal testing should not be done *if* there are no alternative methods and the second reason shows that there *are* alternative methods.)

ACTIVITY 6

In each of the following arguments, there are two reasons and a conclusion. Identify these three parts and state if the reasons are acting independently or jointly.

a) Gas is an inexpensive way to heat your home. Gas heating boilers are small and neat. You should install gas central heating to heat your home.

b) Spending a long time in front of a computer screen can cause eye strain. You've been working on your homework on the computer for several hours. You should have a break from the computer.

c) Hair dye can ruin the condition of hair. You have had your hair dyed several times recently. You would be wise to use conditioner to improve the condition of your hair.

ACTIVITY 7

See if you can write some of your own arguments using two reasons and a conclusion. Then state whether your reasons are acting independently or jointly.

Using diagrams to represent simple arguments

It is often useful to draw a diagram of an argument in order to see how the various parts work together. This section will introduce the idea so that we can then use the approach more extensively in Chapter 3 onwards. Argument diagrams contain the following basic features:

- Shorthand – R and C, etc. to represent the parts (reasons, conclusions, etc.) of the argument.
- Arrows to show the link between a reason and a conclusion.
- + and a line underneath are used to show reasons that jointly support a conclusion.

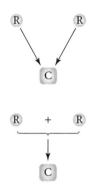

We can demonstrate this by returning to the two arguments about animal experiments. The diagram to the left represents the first argument with two reasons that independently support the conclusion. Note the two arrows that show that *either* reason supports the conclusion

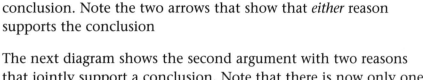

The next diagram shows the second argument with two reasons that jointly support a conclusion. Note that there is now only one arrow, showing that *both* reasons are needed to support the conclusion.

> **KEY TERMS**
>
> **Intermediate conclusion** – a conclusion that is formed on the way to the main conclusion. The intermediate conclusion is still supported by reasons

Intermediate conclusions in longer arguments

Arguments are often longer and more complicated than the ones that we have examined so far. Many longer arguments contain an **intermediate conclusion** before the main conclusion (see also Chapters 3 and 6).

Have a look at this example:

> *Very cold winters lead to high numbers of elderly people needing to be admitted to hospital.*
>
> *We are expecting a very cold winter.*
>
> *So we should expect high numbers of elderly people needing to be admitted to hospital.*
>
> *We will need to make sure that we have enough hospital beds to meet demand.*

In this example, the third statement is in the form of a conclusion, indicated by the word 'so'. However, the argument continues to a fourth statement. The third statement is therefore an intermediate conclusion, which is supported by the first two statements.

> **KEY TERMS**
>
> **Main (or overall) conclusion** – the most important conclusion of an argument. There may be one or more intermediate conclusions before a main conclusion

Every intermediate conclusion then goes on to act as support for the next stage of the argument – it acts like a reason for the **main** or **overall conclusion**.

We indicate the parts of the above argument like this (note the abbreviation IC for 'intermediate conclusion'):

> R1   Very cold winters lead to high numbers of elderly people needing to be admitted to hospital.
>
> R2   We are expecting a very cold winter.
>
> IC   So we should expect high numbers of elderly people needing to be admitted to hospital.
>
> C   We will need to make sure that we have enough hospital beds to meet demand.

! REMEMBER
Remember that **intermediate conclusions** are supported by reasons. An intermediate conclusion acts as a reason for the final conclusion.

Identifying the difference between an intermediate conclusion and the main conclusion

Several types of exam question will require you to identify and distinguish between intermediate and main conclusions. There are two steps in this process.

Step 1

Identify all the conclusions present by using the 'therefore' approach (see page 14) or by looking for other conclusion indicator words.

Look at the following example:

> Raj wants to audition for a local rock band. He plays guitar but is also a good drummer. The band plays gigs all over the city and therefore Raj would need a car to transport his drum kit around with him to gigs. Raj does not have enough money to buy a car and consequently it might be better if he auditioned on guitar.

There are two statements here in the form of conclusions, signalled by 'therefore' and 'consequently':

> 1 Therefore Raj would need a car to transport his drum kit around with him to gigs.
>
> 2 Consequently he might be better to audition on guitar.

Step 2

The next step is to decide which of the statements supports the other.

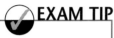

EXAM TIP

The intermediate conclusion will always offer support for the main conclusion. Check this by swapping them around and seeing if the argument makes sense. (It shouldn't.)

In the above example, the need for a car and the fact that Raj doesn't have enough money to get one clearly suggest a problem in becoming the band's drummer. They give support (jointly) for the *main conclusion* – that he should consider auditioning on guitar. The *intermediate conclusion* is (1) above – that he would need a car to transport his kit around – because this statement lends support to the final conclusion.

Now go back and check that the argument doesn't work the other way around to make sure you've got the right answer. Suggesting that Raj should audition on guitar, and the fact that he does not have enough money to buy a car, does not support a main conclusion that he will need a car to transport his kit around with him.

Finally, then, the argument is:

R1   *Raj wants to audition for a local rock band.*

R2   *He plays guitar but is also a good drummer.*

R3   *The band play gigs all over the city.*

IC   *Raj will need a car to transport his drum kit around with him to gigs.*

R4   *Raj does not have enough money to buy a car.*

C   *It might be better if he auditioned on guitar.*

This example also shows us that there may be other reasons used, in combination with the intermediate conclusion (IC), to support the main conclusion (C). Here, both the intermediate conclusion and R4 support the main conclusion.

ACTIVITY ⑧

This is a good chance to practise all the skills that we have looked at so far. For each of the following short passages, identify all the reasons, the intermediate conclusion and the main conclusion.

a) Coffee contains caffeine, which is a stimulant. Taking any stimulant before going to bed stops you from sleeping soundly and so drinking coffee before going to bed will stop you from sleeping soundly. A poor night's sleep may lead you to feel tired in the morning. Therefore drinking coffee before going to bed may cause you to feel tired in the morning.

b) Heather and Bill have been living together for five years. They plan to keep their relationship healthy by taking up new activities and interests as well as setting aside time to discuss their relationship. They have in place good strategies to help them in the future. Many experts suggest that happy relationships rely on just these types of strategies. It is therefore likely that Heather and Bill will continue to live together happily.

c) To stay healthy you are advised to have five portions of fresh fruit or vegetables each day. You have only had four so far today so you should have a piece of fruit. We only have apples and oranges and you do not like oranges, so you should have an apple to maintain your good health.

Explanations and arguments in longer passages

On page 8 we noted how arguments and explanations were two quite different ideas. Arguments contain one or more reasons that support a conclusion which is intended to persuade us of some point of view, idea or suggest a course of action. Explanations, on the other hand, are concerned with information or ideas that are not open to any dispute. Reasons are given for why or how that situation is as it is.

When we meet an explanation, we must identify the situation that is taken for granted and identify the reason or reasons that form the explanation. See how this works in the following example:

> *Mr. Patel's company, Traxter, has just been given the Investors in People award. Mr. Patel puts the success down to regular meetings with his staff and a variety of other staff benefits, such as medical insurance and flexible working hours. Mr. Patel stressed that all staff needed positive encouragement.*

We are told that Mr. Patel's company has been given a prestigious award. There is no need to persuade anyone of this fact and we take it as stated. The reasons that we are given for this success are:

R1 Regular meetings with staff
R2 A variety of other staff benefits
R3 Giving staff encouragement.

In longer passages we must still make a distinction between arguments and explanations, but we may find both in a single passage. Consider the following example:

> *Lots of us like to watch films but sadly cinema audiences have declined because high prices have put people off going and the fact that most cinemas are now out of town means that many youngsters cannot get to them. However, there is really no replacement for seeing a film at the cinema – the sense of occasion, huge screens and better picture quality make the experience special and allow a director's and actors' work to be seen in its proper place.*
>
> *It is such a shame that more people do not enjoy this experience and we should do everything that we can to make the cinema more popular. Building cinemas in town centres and reducing ticket prices is a must if we want a vibrant cinema culture.*

Increasing crowds like these is a must

This is a longer passage and at first sight might seem a bit confusing. Hopefully, as you read it you will 'feel' that there is an argument present – an argument that concludes that we must build cinemas in town centres and reduce ticket prices if we want a vibrant cinema culture. Overall, the argument looks like this:

> R1 Cinema audiences have declined because of high prices and out of town cinemas.
>
> R2 There is no replacement for the special experience of seeing a film at the cinema.
>
> R3 Cinemas allow a director's and actors' work to be seen in its proper place.
>
> R4 We should do everything that we can to make cinema more popular.
>
> C Building cinemas in town centres and reducing ticket prices is a must if we want a vibrant cinema culture.

But now, have a closer look at reason one. Within this reason, there is an explanation at work! We are given an explanation for the decline of cinema audiences – it accounts for this decline by giving two reasons – that people are put off by high prices, and young people are unable to get to out of town cinemas. In this case, however, the reasons form part of an explanation. So the explanation looks like this:

> Cinema audiences have declined.
>
> R1 High prices have put people off going.
>
> R2 Young people are unable to get to out of town cinemas.

So, although the passage overall is an argument heading towards a clearly stated conclusion, there is still room for an explanation along the way. We will look at longer passages in more detail in Chapter 3, but it is important to recognise at this stage that a piece of text may contain both an argument and an explanation.

SUMMARY

At the end of this chapter you should:

- Know that arguments consist of reasons and conclusions
- Know that arguments are persuasive and distinct from opinions and explanations
- Be able to define the terms reason, intermediate conclusion and main or overall conclusion
- Be able to define the term explanation
- Be able to identify reasons and the conclusion in simple arguments
- Be able to distinguish between several reasons that act together jointly in support of a conclusion and several reasons that act independently in support of a conclusion
- Be able to distinguish between intermediate conclusions and main or overall conclusions in longer passages
- Be able to distinguish between arguments and explanations in longer passages.

Assumptions

What are assumptions?

Assumption is another of those words that has an everyday meaning and a much more precise meaning in Critical Thinking.

In everyday life we use the word 'assumption' to refer to something that we say that may or may not be true. For instance, someone might say:

> *I assume it will be good fun at university because my older sister really enjoyed her time there.*

In this case the idea of having a good time is assumed and clearly may or may not be true.

In Critical Thinking, however, we use the word 'assumption' to mean part of an argument that is not stated, but is needed in order for the argument to work – for it to make sense. For instance, have a look at this argument:

> *Young people are not very interested in politics and tend not to vote. Most people who do vote are older, well-off people. Governments tend to represent the interests of those who have voted for them. Elected governments, therefore, do not represent all sections of society. Politicians should change their approach to ensure that more young people vote.*

This argument rests on the idea that governments should represent all sections of society. (After all, if the current situation were acceptable, then the writer (or speaker) would not want politicians to change it.) In other words, the argument relies on an assumption that governments should represent all sections of society.

This example also shows that an assumption is part of the structure of an argument. To be more precise: assumptions are a missing step in the argument, a missing reason that the argument needs in order to support the conclusion. You can see this more clearly if we write the assumption into the argument, as follows:

R1 *Young people are not very interested in politics and tend not to vote.*

R2 *Most people who do vote are older, well-off people.*

R3 *Governments tend to represent the interests of those who have voted for them.*

IC *Elected governments, therefore, do not represent all sections of society.*

R4 *[assumption] Governments should represent all sections of society.*

C *Politicians should change their approach to ensure that more young people vote.*

The assumption that acts as the fourth (unstated) reason in the argument above is very different from the everyday use of the word assumption, which may look like this:

You are just assuming that young people are not interested in politics, when in fact they might be.

EXAM TIP

Finding assumptions is a very important skill in Critical Thinking and one that is often tested in exams. It is also one of the skills that students can find difficult to grasp at first. Allow time to build up your skills – this section will introduce extra refinements and skills as you work through it.

This is not what Critical Thinking defines as an assumption. It is a statement that questions the truth of the sentence 'Young people are not very interested in politics' by suggesting that young people may indeed be interested in politics. It is not a missing part of the argument.

Let's look at a couple of more examples that show how arguments may need an assumption.

1 *Advances in fertility treatments will soon allow parents to choose the sex of their child. This will have serious consequences for society, as there will be more unemployed young men and, as most car accidents are caused by young men, the number of car accidents will rise.*

2 *It has been found that there is a connection between schools that have specialist subject status – such as specialist language or technology colleges – and high academic standards. Interestingly, this connection applies to all their subjects and not just to the specialist subject. We need our young people to achieve higher standards in order to compete in a global economy. We therefore need to ensure that all our schools have specialist subject status.*

The first passage links choice about the sex of a child to problems related to having more boys than girls. The argument therefore rests on the idea that parents will choose boys in preference to girls.

We would say that the assumption is that parents would choose boys in preference to girls if they are allowed to choose the sex of their child. You may have realised this without even thinking about it, but the key point is that the argument falls to pieces without this assumption.

In the second passage, specialist subject status has been related to higher standards. However, it is not clear whether higher standards *result from* the specialist status or whether high achieving schools *have been given* specialist status. Given that there is a recommendation that we should have more specialist schools, the author clearly assumes that high standards result from specialist status rather than the other way around.

REMEMBER

Remember that assumptions are not stated in the passage.

We would say that this is the assumption: becoming a specialist subject school will lead to higher standards in all subjects.

ACTIVITY ⑨

Find an assumption in each of the following short arguments, some of which you have already come across in Chapter 1.

a) Gas is an inexpensive way to heat your home. Gas heating boilers are small and neat. You should install gas central heating to heat your home.

b) Raj wants to audition for a local rock band. He plays guitar but is also a good drummer. The band plays gigs all over the city and therefore Raj would need a car to transport his drum kit around with him to gigs. Raj does not have enough money to buy a car and consequently it might be better if he auditioned on guitar.

c) The traffic is unusually heavy today. It is very important that you get to school on time. You should catch an earlier bus than usual.

Common mistakes in finding assumptions in simple arguments

This section will help you to refine your skills now that you know how we define what assumptions are. We will begin by showing you some common mistakes to illustrate what *not* to do. The example below is adapted from a previous exam paper.

> *If the Met Office's powerful computers cannot make correct weather forecasts four days ahead, how can we trust computer prophecies that global warming will result in a sweaty and ruinous decline in two centuries' time? We only need remember the hurricane of 1987 that the weather forecasters missed only hours before it hit Britain as an example of their inability to forecast the weather.*

Common mistake 1

A very common mistake is finding statements that are not in the passage, but which are not assumptions needed by the argument. For example, you may be tempted to say this about the argument above:

> The author must assume that computers are the only method of forecasting the weather.

This seems reasonable at first sight, as you may think that there are other, and better, methods of forecasting the weather. However, the author does not need to assume this. The author is only arguing

about the accuracy of *computer* predictions of disasters resulting from global warming, not any other methods of predicting, such as evidence from animal behaviour.

! REMEMBER

An assumption must be a missing step in the argument, not just a statement that is not in the text. The argument will not work without the assumption.

The statement that 'computers are the only method of forecasting the weather', therefore, is not in the passage, but ultimately it is not needed by the argument.

Common mistake 2

Students often identify assumptions that appear not to be in the argument at first sight, but on closer inspection are in the argument. They therefore do not fit our criterion of being a missing part of the argument.

For example, you may be tempted to say this about the above argument:

> The author assumes that the Met Office is not very good at making weather forecasts.

! REMEMBER

Before you write down your assumption on an exam paper, check that you have not picked something that is in the passage but phrased it differently.

This statement is certainly in a different language from that of the original short passage, but doesn't tell us anything new. The author has already told us that the Met Office cannot make accurate forecasts four days ahead, so the 'assumption' above is only turning that point of view into a more general comment. It adds nothing to the argument and is not an assumption.

Common mistake 3

Statements that are definitions, or that clarify our understanding of terms, may well help an argument, but they are not assumptions.

For example, you might be tempted to say that this is an assumption in the argument above:

> The Met Office consists of a group of people with training in weather and climate who make weather forecasts.

It is, of course, entirely possible that some people do not know what the Met Office is. Clearly we can work it out to some extent from the context, but we should be clear that this type of clarification is not an assumption.

Correct answers

Now that we've identified common mistakes in finding assumptions, we will move on to look at how to find and correctly phrase assumptions. If we read the passage carefully, we can see that the author moves from the failure of the Met Office's computers to predict the weather to a general point about all computer prophecies. Clearly there may be other computers (used by other organisations, or in other countries) that also predict the weather.

For the argument to work, therefore, we need this assumption:

> *The Met Office's computers are typical of/similar to all powerful weather forecasting computers.*

Or, phrased slightly differently:

> *The author must assume that there are not more powerful or better weather forecasting computers than those used by the Met Office.*

Without this assumption, the author's argument does not work, since there could be other computers out there that are accurately predicting the weather that we *can* trust on global warming. (This is an example of using the 'reverse test', which is described in more detail on pages 35–36.)

There may be further assumptions needed to make the argument work – it is not always the case that there is only one. Can you see why the argument also needs the following assumptions:

> The author must assume that the failure to predict the hurricane was typical of their failure to accurately forecast the weather.
>
> The author must assume that the 1987 hurricane wasn't very unusual/much more difficult to predict than normal weather patterns.

ⓘ REMEMBER

There may be more than one assumption in an argument.

A worked example

For our final practice, here is a worked example of a multiple choice question that illustrates the issues above.

> ## QUESTION
>
> **Read the following passage and then answer the question that follows it.**
>
> > *Recent research has shown that a foetus can hear at 30 weeks old. Computer-generated white noise was played to foetuses between 23 and 34 weeks old. Ultrasound scanning did not pick up any response under 30 weeks old, but it did detect heart and movement responses in the 30–34-week-olds. This fits with the fact that a baby's hearing develops in the 30–34 week period. Given this new knowledge, we should encourage pregnant women to play music to their babies.*
>
> **Which of the following is an underlying assumption of the above argument?**
>
> A Heart and movement responses cannot be detected in foetuses under 30 weeks old.
>
> B Foetuses over 30 weeks old can distinguish between different types of sound.
>
> C Foetuses are particularly responsive to computer-generated white noise.
>
> D Hearing sounds such as music is beneficial to a foetus of at least 30 weeks old.

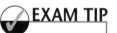

EXAM TIP

Before thinking about a possible assumption, make sure that you have identified the conclusion of the argument. Any assumption that you find must give support to this conclusion.

First of all, we need to identify the conclusion of the argument. The author argues that we should encourage pregnant women to play music to their babies. Any assumption that we find, therefore, must support this conclusion.

It is not A. This statement is not in the passage, in that we know that we can detect movement in the 30–34-week-old foetuses but not what the results were below this age. However, even if this statement were true, it would tell us nothing about whether or not we should encourage women to play music to their babies. It is a statement that is not in the passage, but it is not a missing step in the argument.

It is not B. The argument is about sound in general; whether particular types of sound can be detected does not really matter. All we need to know is that babies can hear, and we are told this in the passage – their hearing develops at 30–34 weeks. This statement, therefore, is not an assumption either.

It is not C. This is a bit like A, in that it may be true or not and is certainly not in the original passage. However, the conclusion is about playing music to babies in the womb, so again we have a statement that is not in the original passage, but is not needed for the argument to work, which means it is not an assumption.

D is the correct answer. By stating that there is a benefit to foetuses we suddenly are given a reason why pregnant women should play music to their unborn babies. This is the missing step in the argument – in other words, the underlying assumption that is needed to make the argument work.

ACTIVITY 10

The following passage is followed by four statements. For each statement explain why it is or is not an assumption needed by the argument in the passage.

a)
> For many years now, Britain has suffered a 'brain drain' of scientists attracted to the rewards of working in other countries. The Government has recently announced that it is investing £1 billion in science to raise scientific salaries to internationally competitive levels. It is also increasing the grant for science PhD students to £11,000. This will stop the brain drain and ensure scientists stay in this country.

A All the best British scientists have gone abroad to work.

B The financial incentive is sufficient to persuade scientists to return to Britain.

C The most important incentive to go to another country is financial.

D Only scientists have been attracted by high financial rewards in other countries.

The importance of accuracy

Having found the assumption, there are several pitfalls to avoid when phrasing (or writing out) your assumption. You may well have done all the right thinking and spotted the missing part of the argument, but you also have to phrase the assumption very accurately so that it exactly fits the needs of the argument.

Two common mistakes in phrasing assumptions are:

- making an assumption too strong
- making an assumption too vague or too weak.

Let's consider the phrasing of assumptions by returning to one of our previous examples.

> *Advances in fertility treatments will soon allow parents to choose the sex of their child. This will have serious consequences for society, as there will be more unemployed young men; and as most car accidents are caused by young men, the number of car accidents will rise.*

What must the author assume in order to argue that allowing parents to choose the sex of their child will have serious consequences for society? There are several possible ways of phrasing an assumption:

1. *All* parents will choose to have a boy if they are allowed to choose the sex of their child.

2. *Some* parents will choose to have a boy if they are allowed to choose the sex of their child.

3. A *significant minority* of parents will choose to have a boy if they are allowed to choose the sex of their child.

4. A *significant majority* of parents will choose to have a boy if they are allowed to choose the sex of their child.

5. A *large number* of parents will choose to have a boy if they are allowed to choose the sex of their child.

All are similar, but which one is right? Let's look at the thinking involved step by step.

Firstly, we need to think very carefully about what the author of this argument is wanting us to accept. The suggestion is that the ability to choose will lead to there being proportionately more boys than there are currently. Presumably there are currently about equal numbers of boys and girls; we need to make sure that our assumption would upset this balance significantly, so that there are quite a lot more boys than girls.

Answers **2** and **5** above would not be enough – 'some' and 'a large number' give us no sense that this would outweigh those choosing to have a girl and result in a significant imbalance. (It is also not clear what 'a large number' means. Is it 100 or 1000 or 10,000? In a country with millions of parents having children, 100 choosing to have a boy would not upset the gender balance.) Both of these versions of the assumption, therefore, are too vague to be correct.

Answers **1** and **3**, on the other hand, are very precise. However, the author suggests the problems stem from having proportionally more boys. They do not need to suggest that *every* baby born would be a boy! This is far too strong for their argument – after all, their argument is still applicable if a handful of girls are born, which immediately shows that 'all' is wrong. We might say that this exaggerates the author's position.

Answer **3** is more tempting, since it is both precise and not 'all'. 'Significant' is a very useful word in assumptions, and in this case it matches the idea that the number of parents who choose to have boys would have to be significant enough to create the problems suggested by the author. However, the answer is then let down by the use of 'minority', as it is possible that this minority would be balanced by a similar number of parents choosing to have a girl.

Realistically, the author needs to assume that more parents will choose to have boys than girls and that the difference will be significant, so that we end up with many more boys, not just one or two. Answer **4** captures this sense – a 'majority' and the helpful 'significant' – to show us that the choice to have boys would be marked enough to produce the social problems suggested.

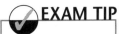
EXAM TIP

There may seem to be a lot of work to do just to get one assumption correct. As you practise, however, you will quickly be able to spot the level of the assumption, so that you do not need to consider all the wrong ones in detail.

Here's one more example:

Graduates from Oxford and Cambridge are still found in senior positions in all the major British institutions. What is less well known is that their salaries are often higher than graduates from other universities who are doing jobs of equivalent status and responsibility. So a place on an Oxford or Cambridge degree course is still a good guarantee of earning more money after university – even if you think that's unfair.

The student is suggesting that a degree from Oxford and Cambridge is enough to lead to a higher salary – not because these people work harder, are better at their jobs or just all round more talented, but because of where they went to university. So the assumption would need to be:

> *The author assumes that graduates from Oxford and Cambridge earn more only because of the fact that they went to Oxford or Cambridge.*

Anything less than this would be too weak and vague as it would allow other possibilities and would not fit with what the author is suggesting.

ACTIVITY 11

Find one assumption in each of the following arguments. Try to make your answers as precise as possible – neither too strong/exaggerated nor too vague.

a)
> **Smoking is a major cause of illness and a considerable strain on the health service's resources. Figures released today show that the number of people giving up smoking has increased, so there will be less strain on the health service. We should be able to use the money saved to improve our preventive treatments.**

b) There are apparently growing concerns about the numbers of 6- and 7-year-olds who are unable to read. However, there is no reason for this to be a problem. Every child has to go to school and is taught by a qualified teacher. Even if this does not work – and apparently it does not always – there are many libraries in our cities with specialist advisers running after school reading clubs and book groups, all designed to help young children read.

c)
"Rugby is a much more exciting game to watch than football. Unlike football it has complex rules and tactics that create many more possibilities, both in attack and defence. Football has much simpler rules and tactics and will never be anything other than boring to watch."

Alex Ridler
Leeds

Checking assumptions: the 'reverse'

How do we know if we have correctly identified an assumption? There are several strategies available, but remember that each situation may require a slightly different approach. One useful tip for checking whether an assumption is necessary for an argument, as opposed to something that the argument does not need, is to use the **reverse test**. This means thinking about the exact opposite of the assumption that you have formed and seeing what impact it has on the argument. If you have the right assumption, the exact reverse should mean that the argument does *not* work.

We can see how this works in our argument about graduates from Oxford and Cambridge (see page 29). We saw that the assumption needed by the author of this argument was the following:

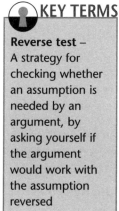

KEY TERMS

Reverse test – A strategy for checking whether an assumption is needed by an argument, by asking yourself if the argument would work with the assumption reversed

> *Graduates from Oxford and Cambridge earn more money only because they went to Oxford and Cambridge.*

Would the argument still work if we reversed the assumption? The statement would then become:

> *Graduates from Oxford and Cambridge do not earn more money (only) because they went to Oxford and Cambridge.*

The argument no longer works, as the assumption now states that going to Oxford or Cambridge is *not* a guarantee of earning more money – which was the point that the author wanted to establish in the first place. Instead, we now have the possibility that they earn more money through working harder or being more skilled.

In short, reversing the assumption and showing that the argument no longer works gives us a very strong indication that our original assumption was correct.

Using the reverse test will also help us identify *incorrect* assumptions. Let's go back to the argument about choosing the sex of our children. One form of the assumption was:

> *Some parents will choose to have a boy if they are allowed to choose the sex of their child.*

The reverse of this would be:

> *Some parents will not choose to have a boy if they are allowed to choose the sex of their child.*
>
> *OR*
>
> *Some parents will choose to have a girl if they are allowed to choose the sex of their child.*

! REMEMBER

Remember, you need to practise the skill of finding assumptions as much as possible to get top marks in the exam.

This reversed statement *does not* upset the argument. The fact that some parents choose to have girls does not affect the author's point that we may end up with problems from having too many boys. The author is not committed to a position that every child will be a boy, so the possibility that some girls are born does not undo the argument. This test, therefore, shows us that the original assumption was incorrectly phrased.

Finally....

Remember that at this stage the skill is to find missing assumptions in an argument. You may be tempted to make a judgement as to whether the assumption is reasonable or not. For the moment, it is best to start with the idea that an assumption is neutral, neither reasonable nor unreasonable. An exam question may ask for an assumption that you consider unreasonable, but this does not mean that it is not the correct answer.

SUMMARY

At the end of this chapter you should:

- Know how the word 'assumption' is used in Critical Thinking

- Be able to distinguish this very specific meaning from everyday uses of the word

- Understand that assumptions are missing steps in arguments

- Understand that not everything that is not stated in a passage is an assumption

- Recognise that the phrasing of an assumption is also important – making sure that your assumptions are neither too specific nor too vague

- Be able to use basic strategies to test if you have got the correct answer when asked to find an assumption – for example, the reverse test

- Keep practising the skills you have learnt.

Applying the skills to longer passages

3

How to approach a longer passage

So far you have practised analysing short arguments, but day to day life often confronts us with longer and more complex arguments. Newspapers try to persuade us to accept certain opinions; television documentaries offer explanations and arguments to convince us to agree with their theories; family and friends want us to see things their way. In your studies, too, you will read arguments and explanations in textbooks, and be expected to use arguments in your essays.

Whether you are looking at a long argument or a short one, you must always identify the main conclusion first. This is important, because your analysis will focus on identifying the reasons that support the conclusion. If you have not identified the conclusion, you are in a poor position to understand how the argument is persuading you to accept it.

! REMEMBER

Always identify the *main conclusion* of the argument first.

A *reason* is that part of an argument which supports the main conclusion by giving you a reason or information which helps you to believe, accept or agree with the conclusion.

Identifying several reasons in a passage

Once you have identified the main conclusion of an argument, you need to look at the reasoning used to support it. A longer argument will have a much more complex structure than the short arguments we have been looking at so far. One way of looking at it is as a group of short arguments which slot together to make one over-arching argument.

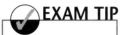

EXAM TIP

In an AS Critical Thinking exam it is likely that each paragraph in a longer passage will be an argument. You will probably need to identify the conclusion of the argument in each paragraph as a reason which supports the main conclusion of the passage. You may also find that one paragraph – normally the first or last – has a further intermediate conclusion and the main conclusion.

! REMEMBER

Remember that an intermediate conclusion is a conclusion which is supported by reasons, and which is itself a reason for the main conclusion.

Each reason should support the main conclusion. The reason may in turn be supported by evidence, examples and other reasons. This means that each reason supporting the main conclusion will in fact be an intermediate conclusion.

Let's identify the reasons in the following long passage. The first thing to do is read the whole passage carefully.

City Choked by Fume Pollution

Three more parts of Southampton have failed to meet government air pollution targets. Town Quay, the junction of Romsey Road and Winchester Road, plus the Winchester Road, Hill Lane and The Avenue area are all being choked by traffic fumes. There are particularly high levels of nitrogen dioxide.

Air pollution is a significant contributor to health problems. Nitrogen dioxide can trigger respiratory problems, especially in children and people with lung problems such as asthma. Research suggests that air pollution in the UK brings forward the deaths of between 12,000 and 24,000 people each year. The elderly and those with lung disease are most at risk.

Traffic levels on roads are constantly rising, and hotter summers, with less wind, result in poorer fume dispersal. This means that levels of dangerous pollutants are rising.

It is clearly important to tackle this problem. People won't leave their cars at home until there are good, reliable alternatives. The first thing to do, therefore, is to get good public transport access for everybody.

Adapted from Southern Daily Echo, *6 June 2005*

The structure of this argument can be analysed as follows:

R1   *Three more parts of Southampton have failed to meet government air pollution targets.*

R2   *Air pollution is a significant contributor to health problems.*

R3   *Levels of dangerous pollutants are rising.*

IC   *(acting as a reason for the main conclusion) It is clearly important to tackle this problem.*

R5   *People won't leave their cars at home until there are good, reliable alternatives.*

C   *The first thing to do, therefore, is to get good public transport access for everybody.*

Diagrams

In Chapter 1 you looked at how to use diagrams to show the structure of a simple argument, with one or two reasons supporting a conclusion. These diagrams can be a useful tool to help you understand the structure of a longer argument.

⚠ REMEMBER

Remember that a diagram is showing a structure of support.

The diagram, on the left for example, shows us that reason 1 supports the conclusion. It does not matter which is written first in the passage; the reason will always be shown first in a diagram, because it supports the conclusion.

We can show the argument about air pollution in a diagram as follows:

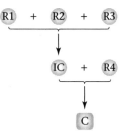

✓ EXAM TIP

Don't worry about diagrams if you find them confusing at this stage. At AS level they are not tested in the exam. They are a useful tool, though, and it is worth persevering with them if you plan to continue with Critical Thinking to A2.

Here we can see that R1, R2 and R3 support the intermediate conclusion jointly. Without R2, neither R1 nor R3 gives us reason to tackle this problem. It is the idea that air pollution contributes to poor health that makes the increase of air pollution a problem at all. IC works jointly with R4 to support the main conclusion. We need to accept both that this is a problem which needs to be tackled, and that a significant cause of this problem (cars) will not go away of its own accord, to justify the conclusion that a particular action should be taken.

The importance of precision

It is important to understand precisely what we are being asked to agree with rather than simply the general drift. It is easy to agree that air pollution is a bad thing and we would be better off without it. This is very general point, which would be accepted by almost everyone. We need to go beyond this general idea, and be precise about what the conclusion of the argument is.

In this case, the author wants us to accept that the first step to take is to get good public transport access for everybody. This statement has three key elements:

- that this course of action is the *first thing* to do
- that public transport access must be *good*
- and that *everybody* must be able to use public transport.

The same point applies to identifying reasons precisely. Let's take R5 as an example: 'People won't leave their cars at home until there are good, reliable alternatives.' If you wrote, 'People won't leave their cars at home,' you would be missing the important suggestion that people would leave their cars at home if there were a good, reliable alternative. And only if they would do this can we draw the conclusion that the first thing to do is to get good public transport access for everybody.

Identifying reasons in a complex structure

In a simple argument it is relatively easy to identify the reasons. For example:

> *Ahmad's old car is dangerously rusty and it breaks down almost every day. He has got a well paid summer job at the local solicitors' office. Ahmad should get a new car.*

In this argument, everything which is not the conclusion is a reason. We can analyse the argument as follows:

> *R1   Ahmad's old car is dangerously rusty.*
>
> *R2   It breaks down almost every day.*
>
> *R3   Ahmad has got a well paid summer job at the local solicitor's office.*
>
> *C   He should get a new car.*

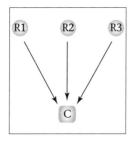

We can also use a diagram to show the structure of this argument (See left):

However, complex arguments also contain evidence, examples and other reasons to support the reasons. 'Climate change is a greater threat than international terrorism.' To give good support to a conclusion like this, an argument is likely to be long, and may have a complex structure.

One common structure is a series of short arguments which slot together to support the overall conclusion.

Reasons in a complex argument like this tend to be *general* statements which give us some reason to believe or agree with the main conclusion. Sentences which contain *specific* examples or statistical information are likely to be evidence which supports the reasons rather than reasons which directly support the main conclusion.

ACTIVITY 12

Read the following passage carefully. Identify the main conclusion and reasons precisely.

We cannot dispute that we need vitamins. It is not a marketing myth but a real need. Vitamins are a small group of substances that are essential in tiny quantities for growth and development.

It is easy to see why many people think that taking vitamin C is as good as eating an apple when it comes to keeping the doctor away.

However, it seems that fruit and vegetables have real benefits over vitamin tablets. Researchers comparing the effects of apples and vitamin C tablets found that apples contain many other chemicals as well as vitamin C, including flavanoids and polyphenols. These are thought to protect against cancer. One of the researchers, Professor Chong Yong Lee, said, 'Some of the chemicals we found in apples are known to be anti-allergenic, some are anti-carcinogenic, anti-inflammatory and anti-viral. Now I have a reason to say an apple a day keeps the doctor away.' Other fruit and vegetables also contain beneficial chemicals which cannot be made into pills.

We don't need to damage our wealth by buying pills to protect our health. Dieticians, nutritionists and other experts agree that apart from small groups of people in special situations, most of us do not need to buy expensive vitamins or food supplements. We can get what we need from a balanced diet.

Mega doses of vitamins can have toxic effects. Some people think that because some is good, more is better, which is not necessarily the case. This is particularly true with vitamins that are fat soluble like vitamin A and will be stored up in the liver. This can reach toxic levels and damage the liver.

> Taking vitamins and food supplements is neither good nor bad but unnecessary for most of us. There is a lot to be said for saving the money and splashing out on a nutritious and delicious well-balanced meal at a ritzy restaurant instead.
>
> *Adapted from*
> *www.netdoctor.co.uk/menshealth/feature/vitamins.htm*

Distinguishing reasons from evidence in a longer passage

As we have seen, reasons are normally general statements used to support a conclusion in an argument. Evidence, on the other hand, is used to support, illustrate or develop a reason. Evidence may be facts that cannot be disputed. More often, the evidence used to support a reason will be information, statistics or scientific data. At this stage we do not need to worry about whether the evidence is true or not. We are considering how this information gives support to reasons *if* it is true.

❗ REMEMBER

Remember that even if the facts can't be wrong, they might not support the argument.

We are concerned with the structure of the argument, and whether the structure is sound. You can have constructions made out of plastic building blocks which are essentially sound, hold together and don't fall over, and others which are badly put together and will never be stable. In the same way, you can have arguments which hold together because they have a solid structure, and others which fall down because of a weak structure.

In the exam, you need to be able to distinguish reasons from evidence. This means separating a reason from the evidence and examples that support it.

Can you identify the evidence in the following argument?

> *'Infomania' can seriously interfere with your performance at work. Research carried out by the Institute of Psychiatry says that distractions caused by emails and telephone calls result in a 10 point IQ drop in the average worker. So, if you want to work at your best, don't constantly check your emails, text and phone messages.*

The evidence here is in the second sentence, as we can see when we analyse the argument:

E   Research carried out by the Institute of Psychiatry says that distractions caused by emails and telephone calls result in a 10 point IQ drop in the average worker.

R   'Infomania' can seriously interfere with your performance at work.

C   So, if you want to work at your best, don't constantly check your emails, text and phone messages.

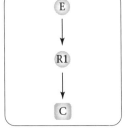

We can draw a diagram of this argument as follows (see left). (Note that in diagrams the evidence (E) is always shown before the reasons, because evidence supports reasons.)

! REMEMBER

Remember, a diagram shows the structure of support in an argument. So we put evidence (E) first in a diagram because it supports a reason, even if the evidence is given after the reason in the passage.

ACTIVITY 13

Look at the following short argument. Identify the evidence used.

a) Students concerned for their long term health should avoid American football, as it is the sport most likely to cause neck injury in the US. Researchers combined hospital admission numbers with sport participation figures across the US in the 1990s. For every 10,000 participants, they found overall neck injuries in 5.85 football players. That's more than the 2.8 hockey players and 1.67 soccer players combined.

(adapted from Focus, *July 2005)*

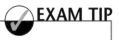
EXAM TIP

When you identify reasons in the exam, make sure that you leave out any examples. You may also need to rephrase slightly if the reason is unclear when taken out of context.

Examples

Examples are a further way of developing a reason. They illustrate the reason, giving a specific situation in which the reason holds. Their purpose, therefore, is to back up the reason, so that it provides good support for the conclusion. There are two main ways of using an example to illustrate a reason. You may simply find a list of specific examples:

Fruit which can be grown in the UK, such as apples, pears, raspberries, gooseberries and strawberries doesn't need to be transported around the world.

The examples strengthen the reason by offering an appropriate image or concrete situation to develop it rather than logical support. The example does not count as part of the reason, even when it is written in the middle of it. Phrasing the reason precisely means leaving out examples. Thus, the reason here is: 'Fruit which can be grown in the UK has many advantages.'

Precise phrasing can also mean a little bit of rewriting. The conclusion of this passage is: 'It is by far the best choice.' However, taken out of context, we do not know what 'it' is, so if you are asked to identify the conclusion of this passage precisely, you would unpack the meaning of 'it' and write: 'Fruit which can be grown in the UK is by far the best choice.'

The second most common kind of example is where a general idea is illustrated through a more developed example:

EXAM TIP

In the exam you may be asked about the use of examples in a passage.

> *You don't have to have a large garden to grow your own food. Many kinds of fruit and vegetable can be grown in containers, which will fit even on a small balcony. For example, Uncle Brian grows potatoes in a dustbin, and tomatoes, chillies, courgettes, aubergines, peas, French beans, strawberries, apples, spinach, rocket and lettuce – all in pots on the patio.*

Here, Uncle Brian is an example which supports the reason by demonstrating that the general statement is not just an abstract idea but has real instances in the real world.

ACTIVITY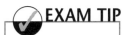

REMEMBER

Remember that analysing an argument is breaking it down into evidence, reasons, intermediate conclusions and conclusion. If you find a reason in each paragraph which supports the main conclusion, you are analysing the longer argument.

Let's practise all the skills you have learnt so far by analysing a longer argument. Read the following passage and identify:

a) the main conclusion

b) the reason in each paragraph which supports the main conclusion

c) the evidence which supports the reasons

d) two examples that the author uses to illustrate the reasons.

Driving skill is an obvious but essential quality in an F1 driver. To achieve the fastest lap times, F1 cars are driven to the limits of safety. Drivers must have split second reaction times to avoid a devastating crash. To maximise speed, they must also place the car centimetre perfect lap after lap. Recent rule changes have reduced downforce, required drivers to use the same tyres for the whole race and to keep the same engine for two race meetings. These changes mean that levels of grip are lower, stopping distances are longer and the cars are far more difficult to drive.

A typical F1 race can last an hour and a half, so drivers need cardiovascular fitness. They also need the strength to deal with turning corners fast. As Jensen Button turns into the flat right-hander at Silverstone's Copse Corner, his neck muscles will be straining to support a weight equivalent to 30 bags of sugar. Pulling 3.5 G through the 150 mph bend, he'll experience lateral forces that are normally only felt by fighter pilots or astronauts. F1 drivers have to be among the very fittest athletes in the world to cope with the incredible strains that full throttle racing can place on the human body.

Drivers must make strategy judgements and fine tune the car settings as they hurtle along at breathtaking speeds of 200 mph or more, so they need to be competent engineers as well. They have to interpret the complex data beamed back to the pits, maintain a conversation with the engineer during the race and make adjustments to the car's brakes, fuel mixture and other settings.

The right mental approach is critical. Drivers need to be self-motivated, have the desire to win, and be able to control their aggression. They have to perform under intense pressure in qualifying and during races. F1 drivers also have to shrug off the real possibility of death or injury. At the 1996 Australian Grand Prix, Martin Brundle (now ITV's F1 commentator) had a huge accident at the start of the race. After he was pulled out of his upturned car, Brundle sprinted down the track to his spare car and started all over again.

Because drivers have to perform all these amazing feats at the same time, at 200 mph, they must surely count amongst the elite of multi-taskers.

Adapted from an article in Focus *no. 152, July 2005*

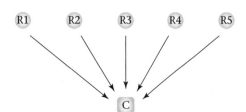

We can see that the argument in the above activity has five reasons which support the main conclusion. We can draw a diagram like the one to the left. (Note that each of the five reasons is supported by other evidence and examples.)

Identifying intermediate and overall conclusions in longer passages

We have seen that reasons which support a main conclusion in a long argument are often intermediate conclusions because they are supported by other reasons, evidence and examples. All the same, we refer to them as reasons because it is also possible to have intermediate conclusions between these reasons and the main conclusion. It is important to understand that a structural element in an argument may have more than one role. It may help to think of a family tree: one individual may be both a mother and a daughter, or a father and a son. Which name you give to them depends on your perspective and which role they are playing at the time.

One common structure for an argument in Critical Thinking exams is:

✓ EXAM TIP

In the exam, you will not necessarily face a passage with five reasons supporting the conclusion. It may have as few as three reasons, or as many as eight.

Five supported reasons which support an intermediate conclusion, which supports the main conclusion. When you are analysing a longer argument like this, it is important to check that you have correctly identified the main and intermediate conclusions. The reasons may all support the intermediate conclusion, but the intermediate conclusion must also support the main conclusion. The main conclusion does not, however, support the intermediate conclusion, and you can check this by swapping them round.

ACTIVITY

Identify the reasons and main conclusion in this argument.

Funding for music lessons in schools is increasingly being squeezed, leaving many children without the opportunity to learn an instrument. This is a disgrace – every child should have this opportunity. Music clearly has a great many benefits.

Because children have to listen carefully to the sounds that they and others are making, and play the right note at the right time, learning a musical instrument can improve their concentration. Research by the Utterly Fictional Primary Music Trust shows that 95% of children who learn an instrument are better focused during other lessons.

EXAM TIP

When you are asked to identify the main conclusion, it can be tempting to go for the intermediate conclusion, because it is often supported by all of the reasons. You have to check for further ideas which are supported by the intermediate conclusion to make sure you really have identified the main conclusion. The trick is to find the idea that is supported by everything else – the main idea that you are supposed to agree with after reading the argument.

Music is based on repeating mathematical patterns. Learning to play an instrument involves a conscious, academic effort to understand these patterns and also an intuitive, emotional, internal understanding of which patterns feel right when played. This improves children's mathematical ability.

Because music accesses our deepest emotions, playing an instrument can also provide a valuable emotional outlet. People who are stressed, sad or excited can play through their emotions, turning them into something beautiful, rather than repressing their feelings or taking them out on friends and family.

Being able to play an instrument is also socially useful. Whether strumming the guitar around the camp fire, banging an old piano in Gran's living room, or playing first violin at the last night of the Proms, a musician can bring joy and focus to any social group. Children can also make new friends and gain confidence and maturity through playing in orchestras, bands and concerts.

Identifying contradictions, inconsistency and counter arguments

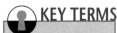

KEY TERMS

Contradiction – bits of the argument that are saying completely opposite things

Inconsistency – bits of the argument that don't work together, as they pull in different directions. They don't have to pull in completely opposite directions, although a contradiction is a special kind of inconsistency

If a short argument includes a **contradiction** or **inconsistency** it is usually easy to spot. For example:

> R1 *Jewellery is fun, attractive and largely harmless.*
>
> R2 *Jewellery is vain adornment which encourages a superficial view of women.*
>
> C *So there is no good reason not to wear jewellery.*

In this argument it is clear that R2 contradicts the statement in R1 that jewellery is largely harmless. It is also clear that R2 provides a good reason (if it is true) not to wear jewellery, so it contradicts the conclusion.

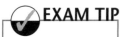

EXAM TIP

In the exam, you may be asked to identify a contradiction or inconsistency in an argument.

See if you can identify the contradiction in this argument:

> *Children don't watch TV instead of running around; they do it instead of other sedentary activities such as reading. Some children spend up to eight hours a day watching television. It's not surprising they don't run around as much as they used to.*

And what is the inconsistency in this argument?

> *We should encourage people not to use cosmetics because they are a means of concealing the true personality. A further reason not to use cosmetics is that they increase our exposure to harmful chemicals. It would be better to use natural alternatives such as lemon juice or aloe vera.*

Inconsistency and contradiction are harder to identify in a longer argument. It may be that two pieces of evidence used to support different reasons are inconsistent, that is, they do not work together. Written down next to each other the difference becomes apparent, but buried in different parts of the argument they may escape notice.

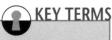

KEY TERMS

Counter argument – an argument that puts forward an opposing line of reasoning. It may be a single counter reason or a short argument with an explicit conclusion. A counter argument is introduced by the author in order to dismiss it, and thus support the author's own argument

Many longer passages also contain a **counter argument**. Although this is an argument that counters, or opposes, the author's conclusion, it is very different from a contradiction or inconsistency. This is because the author introduces the counter argument in order to dismiss it – it therefore acts ultimately to support their own conclusion. Inconsistency and contradiction are weaknesses in the argument, whereas the author's use of a counter argument may well strengthen the argument.

Look at this example of a counter argument:

> *We would be better off without modern gadgets. We waste a huge amount of money on them. **It is commonly thought that they save time and labour,** but we spend so much time choosing them, shopping for them and fixing them, that we actually spend more time and effort on the gadgets than we would have spent on the tasks they do.*

The part of the argument **in italics** puts forward a point of view which disagrees with the conclusion, and then says why it is wrong. This makes it a counter argument.

ACTIVITY ⓰

Identify any contradiction, inconsistency and counter argument in the passage below.

Fit For Life Health Centre – our core beliefs

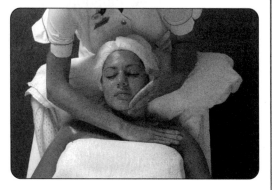

We should embrace the many advantages offered by the health and beauty industry as it clearly has so many benefits for the individual and society.

Looking good has important consequences for the way we feel. You cannot achieve inner serenity if your hair, nails and skin are not perfect. Yoga is nothing to a good manicure. Knowing that your muscle tone is just right can give you the confidence to don that Lycra.

Exercise is the best way to improve the way you feel about yourself. It releases serotonin in the brain which promotes feelings of happiness. The best way to get exercise is to join a gym and work with a personal trainer. This can be excellent value for money at around £120 a month.

Some people may prefer to walk their dogs or cycle, but this is a hugely selfish attitude. They end up dirty and smelly, which offends those of us with an appreciation of beauty. They are also wilfully refusing to contribute to the employment of beauty and fitness experts, who play an important part in the modern economy. It doesn't make sense to reject the many facilities offered by a health and fitness centre.

Image isn't everything. People should learn to be happy with the way they are, and we should all learn to value people's deeper qualities rather than sneering at their imperfect, blobby bodies. Deep acceptance of ourselves can best be achieved by working with what we have at a health centre.

Fit for home, fit for work – Fit For Life

Assumptions in longer passages

You looked at assumptions in short arguments in Chapter 2. Assumptions are important steps on the way to justifying the conclusion. To identify an assumption you can ask yourself, 'What else do I have to agree with, if I'm going to agree with the conclusion?'

Assumptions can be found at every stage of an argument. They can be made between evidence and reasons, between reasons and intermediate conclusions and between intermediate conclusions and the main conclusion.

! REMEMBER

Assumptions are unstated parts of an argument. This means that they are not written down. If you find yourself copying something from the page, it is not an assumption.

ACTIVITY

✔ EXAM TIP

When looking at a long passage, break it down into shorter arguments, and look for the missing steps. Keep asking yourself if there is anything else you have to agree to between the stated parts of the argument. Be precise, and work through the text statement by statement, paragraph by paragraph, looking for the missing links.

Identify any unstated, underlying assumptions in the following passage.

International travel is killing the world. Every passenger on a return flight from London to New York discharges the equivalent of 3 tonnes of carbon dioxide. Carbon dioxide released by aircraft represents about 5% of our total emissions.

Flights are unrealistically cheap so we cannot resist them. Air travel soared by almost 70% between 1990 and 2002. The airline industry is currently growing by about 6% and the government plans to increase capacity at London's three airports. Something needs to be done about this uncontrollable growth.

All this travel is unnecessary. In today's world there is no business deal that cannot be sealed by email or telephone conversation. There is no need for a physical presence in Bangkok or Melbourne.

There is clearly no good reason for international travel. So we should support plans to tax aviation fuel so heavily that international travel will become economically unviable.

✓ EXAM TIP

In the exam there are likely to be multiple choice questions asking you to draw a conclusion from a piece of reasoning or evidence. There may also be questions in section B which ask you to draw further or alternative conclusions from the evidence or reasoning in the longer passage.

Drawing conclusions

We have looked at evidence and examples supporting reasons, and reasons providing support for conclusions. The same skills allow us to look at reasons, evidence and examples and draw conclusions from them, that is, decide which conclusions can be supported by this reasoning.

Take the following example:

> *Rabbits are soft, furry, grey creatures with long ears.*
> *Daisy is soft, furry and grey. She has long ears.*
> *What can we conclude about Daisy?*
>
> *a) Daisy must be a rabbit.*
>
> *b) Daisy cannot be a rabbit.*
>
> *c) Daisy may be a rabbit.*

We know that Daisy shares four characteristics with a rabbit. We do not know anything else about her. We know nothing to suggest that she cannot be a rabbit, so we can exclude b) as an answer. On the other hand, extra information may reveal that she brays. So we cannot be sure that she must be a rabbit – other creatures are soft, grey and furry with long ears. Thus we can conclude that Daisy *may* be a rabbit.

ACTIVITY ⓲

What conclusions can you draw from the following?

a) **I need to wash up and take the dog for a walk. The forecast is for rain later this morning.**

b) **Girls aged 13–15 spent an average £5.30 a week on clothing and footwear in 2003. This was a quarter of their weekly spend and double the £2.50 spent by boys. Girls in this age group spent an average of just 50p on games, toys, hobbies and pets, while boys spent £2.60 on this.**

c) **Between 1971 and 2003 the number of people aged 65 and over rose by 28% while the number of under 16s fell by 18%.**

For d and e, pick the conclusion best supported by the evidence and reasons.

d) Diving requires grace, elegance, strength and courage. Gina has all these qualities.

    1. Gina will be a fantastic diver.

    2. Gina may well have the potential to be a good diver.

    3. Gina should learn to swim.

e) We have had trouble getting our wireless network to work, even though it was recommended on the website. Dave had trouble getting his wireless network to work, even though he writes computer software. This technology is developing fast.

    1. Current wireless networks are rubbish.

    2. Don't buy a wireless network.

    3. It may be worth waiting for improvements before buying a wireless network.

SUMMARY

You should now be able to:

- Analyse the structure of a longer passage, identifying reasons, evidence, unstated assumptions, intermediate conclusions and the main conclusion.

- Understand structure diagrams when other people use them.

- Identify inconsistency, contradiction and counter arguments and distinguish between them.

- Draw conclusions from evidence and short passages of reasoning.

Evaluating evidence: asking the right questions

4

! REMEMBER

Evidence may be facts that cannot be disputed, or information, statistics or scientific data which are not always obviously true.

In the next two chapters we turn to the evaluation of arguments. Evaluating an argument means deciding whether it works well – whether it is a **strong argument** or a **weak argument**. In Chapter 4 we will consider the use of evidence. In Chapter 5 we will consider technical flaws in the pattern of reasoning.

Types of evidence

There are many forms of evidence. If you wanted to choose a further education college, for example, you might look at the results data, the range of courses on offer, the number of clubs, the kind of parties, the support systems available if you have academic or personal problems and students' opinions. All of these would count as evidence.

It is often neater and quicker to present evidence numerically. For example, we do not necessarily want to read what every student thinks of a college: knowing that 93% of students would recommend the college to others is enough. However, the way in which evidence is simplified, or converted into numerical form, can present problems. We will therefore look closely at two common ways of presenting numerical evidence, percentages and averages.

When evaluating the use of evidence, the trick is to ask the right questions. We are not concerned with the truth of the evidence, but with how well it supports the reasons *if* it is true. Evidence must be meaningful, relevant, representative and reliable.

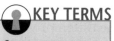

KEY TERMS

Strong argument – an argument with a solid structure, which uses evidence and examples that are precisely relevant and which supports the conclusion successfully

Weak argument – an argument which may contain many flaws, use evidence that is irrelevant or poorly sourced and which provides limited support for the conclusion

Is it meaningful?

'According to Mensa, the society for people with high IQs, one person in 50 will be in the top 2% in terms of IQ.' This is not meaningful evidence. 2% means two in 100, which can also be expressed as one in 50. It might be useful to remind us of this, if our basic maths is a bit shaky, but it is not meaningful. By contrast, the information that 2% of the population have one green eye and one blue would mean something, whether or not it is true.

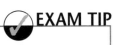

EXAM TIP

In the exam you may have to answer multiple choice questions which ask which piece of evidence, if true, would strengthen or weaken a particular conclusion.

You may also be asked in Section B to identify strength and weakness. That is, you should be able to say that a piece of evidence is strong because it is precisely relevant to the reasoning, representative and reliable, or that it is weak because it is too vague, unrepresentative or unreliable.

KEY TERMS

Mean – the mean of a set of data is the sum of all the individual figures divided by the number of individual items

Median – the median of a set of data is the middle value when the data are arranged in order

Mode – the mode of a set of data is the figure which occurs most frequently

Percentages are a valuable tool for presenting evidence or data. However, they are often abused and may become meaningless. For example, headlines may tell us that violent crime has risen by 100%. This needs to be set in context to be meaningful. We could consider a rise from one incidence of violence in the UK to two. This would be a 100% increase. Millions of people live in the UK, so this rise from one to two would not be significant. A move from 30 teenage muggings to 60 in a small town would be more significant.

We may be told that a particular washing powder is 50% more effective. We need to ask 'more effective *than what*'? Is it 50% more muddy water?

When looking at averages, we also need to question what we mean. When we say 'average' we generally mean normal, middle of the road, unexceptional. When we are evaluating the use of averages as evidence, however, we need to be aware that there are three commonly used kinds of average: **mean**, **median** and **mode**.

There can be three different averages for a set of data. For example:

> *Nine people take a test, and their results are as follows:*
> *40%, 45%, 45%, 45%, 49%, 52%, 53%, 59%, 99%*

The mean is 54%. The median, or mid-point, is 49%. The mode, the most commonly occurring value, is 45%. These different averages can be used in different ways. A newspaper editor might take the mean and gleefully pronounce that 78% of these students are under average. The teacher might use the mode, and declare defiantly that 89% of the students are average or above average. Both of them are right, in their own terms. We need to set these averages in context for this evidence to be meaningful.

Relevant

Relevant evidence is precisely focussed on the reason it supports. It must cover the same area and timescale as the reasoning and not leave gaps in our knowledge. Information about the general topic is

relevant evidence in the everyday sense of 'relevance', but is not precise enough to be relevant to the reasoning in the critical thinking sense.

For example, if we are considering what evidence we need to support a claim that 'Hawkwood Towers is a good college', we might look at:

- 'Hawkwood Towers is one of four colleges in town,' and
- '80% of students achieve at least one AB grade at AS level.'

The first piece of evidence is on the same topic of colleges, but it is not precisely relevant to our claim that Hawkwood Towers is a good college. The second piece of evidence is precisely relevant: it supports the idea that Hawkwood Towers is a good college.

Let's take another example:

> *Lemar collected awards for Best Album and Act of the Year at the MOBO Awards in 2005. This shows that he is one of the strongest British musicians.*

The evidence is about the Music of Black Origin awards in one year. It is too limited to tell us that Lemar is now one of the strongest British musicians. He may be, but we can't tell how he fares against non-Mobo artists. There are gaps in our knowledge.

ACTIVITY ⑲

Evaluate the evidence in the following passages:

a) **'Crime rises again! The number of people in prison has risen by 20%.'**

b) **'It no longer makes economic sense for families to provide their own vegetables. The modern day supermarket offers vegetables at a price that undercuts the cost of growing them for yourself. Marina Kiblitskaya found that people in Russia spent considerably more money growing their own vegetables than if they had purchased them in markets.'**

Extract taken from OCR's As Level Critical Thinking Paper, May 2003

Representative

We have to question whether evidence is based on a representative sample. Let's say that we survey a class of 30 children, and find

that 12 of them are blonde, six have brown hair, six have red hair and six black hair. We can happily conclude that 40% of the class are blonde, and 20% respectively brown, red and black. We can't, however, extend this to the whole population, or even conclude that another class in the same school will have a similar distribution of hair colour. So whenever we look at evidence, we should ask ourselves whether the group it is based on is typical or representative of the wider group it is being applied to.

We must also be careful about applying a statistic which represents the population as a whole to a small group. Suppose we knew that 60% of the UK population had brown eyes. We could not then conclude that exactly 60% of the people in your class have brown eyes.

What questions might we ask about the following evidence before we draw any conclusions?

> *Researchers who worked with families and day care centres have suggested that children who stay at home with a parent until they are two and a half achieve higher levels in standard tests when they are seven than children who attend day care centres.*

These are some of the questions that we could ask:

- Who funded the research?
- How many children were sampled? Two or two thousand?
- Were the day care centres in similar social areas to the children at home?
- How well educated were the parents and day care workers?
- How did the researchers get access to the children? Presumably they could only work with parents who were willing to take part in the study. These would probably be people who were happy with their role at home.

The answer to any of these questions may make the sample unrepresentative, even if the survey was otherwise well designed. For example, if researchers could only work with parents who were willing to take part in the study, we would then only be able to conclude that there is an academic advantage for a child who remains at home with a parent who is happy to be there. We could not conclude that all toddlers are better off cared for at home.

ACTIVITY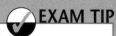

✓ EXAM TIP

If you are uncomfortable with numbers, don't panic. You will not have to do calculations in the exam. You will only need to understand some of the ways in which numbers can be used to represent (or misrepresent) things.

Evaluate the use of evidence in these passages by asking questions.

> a) 95% of Americans think George Bush is a wonderful president, according to a recent poll. This survey was conducted in shopping malls in Texas during normal working hours.

> b) According to Mensa, one person in every fifty will be in the top 2%. So if you know 150 people, three of them are intelligent enough to be in Mensa.

> c) People were asked to name their favourite National Trust coastline in a survey. The white cliffs of Dover were runaway winners with 22% of votes.

We also need to remember that, although most of us are normal, very few of us are exactly average. So if we are given evidence about an average, we cannot draw conclusions that apply the average to everyone, or to one particular individual. An average represents a mid-point rather than being representative of everyone in the group.

ACTIVITY ㉑

Evaluate the evidence in the following passage:

'The average amount spent on lottery tickets is about £3 a week. This represents only 0.65% of the average income in Britain. Such a small amount completely undermines the idea that expenditure on the lottery is at the expense of more important and essential items such as nutritious food.'

Extract taken from OCR's As Level Critical Thinking Paper, January 2004.

Reliable

You have considered some of the criteria that make evidence reliable in Unit 1. Reliable evidence should come from a source which is reputable, authoritative and without a clear motive to mislead, such as vested interest or bias. Statistics and other numerical evidence can mislead even if there is no vested interest involved. Often such evidence is simply misused. We need to ask what is being hidden by the evidence, what isn't being said, what is being twisted or manipulated, and what has been discarded because it did not fit the aims of the researchers.

If we are told that 'many people' support a particular measure, it is worth asking for the precise figures. It may turn out that 37% of people asked said they did agree, 39% didn't agree, and the rest didn't know. The reporters are not lying by saying that many people support the measure, but they are not giving us the whole picture either.

Again, watch out for reports which tell you that most people are against something. It may well turn out that 51% were against it and 49% would support it. Although it is technically true that a majority were against, it would be more accurate to say that opinion was divided almost equally on this matter.

Let's look at an example of evidence being ignored:

Red wine is good for your health

A study has found that red wine is a rich source of polyphenols, which are linked to long life. They also have an anti-oxidant effect which combats cancer and heart disease. We should clearly ditch the guilt and savour a health-giving glass or two.

This argument has ignored the wealth of evidence about the damage done to our health by the alcohol in the red wine, especially when drunk to excess. This evidence is well known to us all. It has also omitted information which is not common

✓ **EXAM TIP**

In the exam you may be expected to judge that a passage which ignores evidence in common knowledge is selective in its use of evidence. You will not be expected to have specialist knowledge.

knowledge. For example, the study linking red wine to long life talks about small quantities of wine; it also suggests that olive oil is just as good; and scientists suggest that the polyphenols in red wine lengthen the life of yeast, not people. So we cannot really conclude that red wine is good for your health. We can only conclude that red wine contains substances which have beneficial effects.

When ignorance, prejudice and several misuses of statistics come together, the result can be conclusions which have no support at all:

Schools failing our children

According to government figures, 20% of children are failing their end of primary school literacy test (SAT). One in five children leaves school unable to read even the label on a jar of food. Even more shocking, less than half of children gain pass marks in all three assessed tasks – reading, writing and numeracy – at the end of primary school. These children are being failed by our schools.

One of the most worrying things about this kind of misuse of statistics is that most of us gain our information from reports such as this in the newspapers, and do not have the background information to correct it. All we can do is question the use of evidence and examples critically.

Examples

For examples to support an argument, they must be typical or representative. If they are unusual, they may work against the argument rather than with it.

Let us look again at the argument about schools failing children who cannot read. We may wish to question whether reading a label on a jar of food is a good indication of literacy. On the surface it seems like a simple task, and it is certainly important to know what

we are eating. However, if we look at a fairly typical jar of pre-cooked supermarket brand pasta sauce, we find information about calorie, fat and carbohydrate content, instructions on how to store it, how to contact the manufacturer, how long it remains safe to eat, where it was produced, how much it weighs, a guide to how long it should be cooked in a variety of ovens and microwaves, a marketing description, a recipe, a warning about heating thoroughly and not reheating, allergy information, instructions for opening the can, a bar code and a list of ingredients which includes technical terms such as 'emulsifying salts' and 'Esters of Diglycerides of Fatty Acids'.

It is likely that only an exceptional 11-year-old could make much of this information. Reading labels on pre-packed food is, therefore, a poor example of what a normal, literate 11-year-old should be able to do.

On the face of it, giving an extreme example may seem very persuasive. Here, the implication is that a child who cannot read food labels must be rubbish at reading. However, extreme examples are often also more open to counter argument. Here, if we can show that children who achieve level 3 in literacy tests can get basic information from a food label, the author has not carried their point. If we can also show that even a child working at level 4 in literacy tests cannot fully read food labels, we may begin to think that the author is ranting rather than arguing.

ACTIVITY ㉒

Evaluate the use of examples in the following passages:

a) We should not reject modern fabrics out of hand. They have many advantages over traditional and natural fibres. Many modern fabrics are easy to wash and care for, and are not ruined as easily as, for example, silk. Furthermore, modern fabrics allow us to adapt to the weather conditions we find. For example, neoprene allows us to engage in water sports throughout the year. It is even possible to go surfing in Scotland in December in a modern wetsuit.

b) Driving a car through London is unbearably slow. It is often quicker to go on foot. Jeremy Clarkson drove from the suburbs to central London in a race with a marathon runner, and lost. We should consider whether a car is really necessary for our journey.

ACTIVITY ㉓

⚠ REMEMBER

Remember to identify the main conclusion.

When evaluating evidence and examples, ask yourself these questions:

- Is the evidence meaningful?

- Is it relevant – precisely focussed on the reasons?

- Is the evidence representative?

- Is the evidence reliable?

- Are the examples typical and relevant?

Evaluate the use of evidence and examples in the following passage.

Having sweated over the origins of the universe and split the atom, academics have finally tackled the question that has perplexed mankind since the dawn of time: what are the best chat up lines?

If a man wants to impress a woman, he needs to let her know with his opening gambit that he is cultured, generous and physically fit, but not boastful.

Psychologists from Edinburgh and Central Lancashire universities tried 40 'verbal signals of genetic quality' on 205 people. Apparently two of the best are, 'It's hot today isn't it? It's the best weather when you're training for the marathon,' and 'The Moonlight Sonata, or to give it its true name, *Sonata quasi una fantasia.* A fittingly beautiful piece for a beautiful lady.'

The Independent on Sunday decided to road test the research at a fashionable bar in London. They began with one of the top five offerings.

'Ten ton polar bear.'

'What?' replied the young brunette at the bar.

'Well, it breaks the ice, doesn't it?' we said optimistically. The verbal response was unprintable. The marathon line attracted only giggles. We were more successful with the line, 'There's something in your eye. Nope, it's just a sparkle.'

The scientists maintain that while it might be good to hint at having the means to support a potential partner, showing off is not appreciated. 'I was just wondering if you had space in your bag for my Merc keys' was their ultimate flop.

Source: Independent on Sunday, *6 November 2005*

Strengthening or weakening an argument

In the exam you are likely to be asked to evaluate the use of evidence and examples in a longer text in section B. Some multiple choice questions may also ask you to identify which piece of evidence, if true, would most strengthen or weaken an argument.

If a piece of evidence supports one of the reasons or the reasoning, then it strengthens the argument. If it supports an opposite conclusion it weakens the argument. It may be neutral or irrelevant and neither strengthen nor weaken the argument.

Once you have considered this, you need to consider whether the evidence is precisely focussed and well used. One of the possible answers may seem to work well, but on closer examination may be focussed on a slightly different conclusion.

It seems that men are primed for parenting. In 2000 a team of researchers at Memorial University in Newfoundland, Canada, revealed that male hormones change when their partners are having a baby. In men who were cohabiting with pregnant women, prolactin, a hormone which promotes fostering behaviour, rose steadily. On average it increased by 20% during the three weeks before their partners gave birth. So parenting is a natural and important part of being a man.

Source: Adapted from New Scientist, *27 August 2005, pp 40–41*

Which of the following, if true, would most weaken the above argument?

A   *At the time of birth, the level of the male hormone, testosterone, dropped by up to 33% in the men studied.*

B   *In the UK 30% of non-resident fathers have no contact with their children.*

C   *Children of 'involved' fathers pass more exams at 16 and are less likely to have a criminal record by age 21.*

D   *When confronted with a crying or smiling baby, fathers and mothers have the same patterns of response as measured by heart rate and blood pressure.*

A would strengthen the argument by giving additional evidence that men have hormonal reactions to birth.

B would most weaken the argument, and is therefore the right answer, as it demonstrates that some men can resist the urge to parent. However, it does not significantly weaken the argument: it does not demonstrate either that men are not primed for parenting or that parenting is not a natural part of being a man.

C would slightly strengthen the argument by showing that active fatherhood is important.

D would also strengthen the argument by showing that mothers and fathers do not react differently to babies.

SUMMARY

You should now be able to:

- Evaluate evidence by asking questions:
  - Is this evidence meaningful?
  - Is it relevant: is it focussed precisely on the reasoning?
  - Is it representative: who was asked? What factors might make a sample distorted?
  - Is this evidence reliable: is the source reputable, authoritative and unbiased? Is the evidence being manipulated? Is it too selective?
- Evaluate examples by asking whether they are typical and relevant.
- Assess whether additional evidence strengthens or weakens an argument.

Evaluating reasoning – flaws

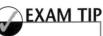

KEY TERMS

Flaw – a fault in the pattern of reasoning which weakens the support given to the conclusion of an argument

EXAM TIP

One of the most important things to remember when evaluating an argument is to look at the pattern of the reasoning. You will not gain marks for simply disagreeing with something the author has written, or providing a counter argument.

KEY TERMS

Appeal to authority – claiming your conclusion must be right because an expert or someone in authority supports it. This is a flaw in reasoning

A **flaw** is a fault in the pattern of reasoning which weakens the support given to the conclusion of an argument. In this chapter you will learn to spot common flaws in reasoning, understand what is wrong with them and explain the problem.

Irrelevant appeals

Many arguments are flawed because they use an irrelevant appeal to support their conclusion, for example the 'appeal to authority', 'appeal to popularity', 'appeal to tradition' and 'appeal to history'. Such appeals do not provide strong support for a conclusion.

Appeal to authority

It is common to claim that your conclusion is right because it is backed by an expert, as if an authority can settle the matter. For example, 'It is right to go to war. The Prime Minister says so.' However, just because someone is an authority, it does not mean that their viewpoint overrides all others. The **appeal to authority** does not quash the validity of strong reasoning: arguments should be evaluated on their merits, not on the authority of the people who use them.

Note that it may be acceptable to quote an authority's evidence or reasons in support of a conclusion. There is an important difference between this and saying your conclusion must be right simply because an authority says so.

> *There should be no exceptions to the ban on smoking in public places because the medical evidence about the damage done by smoking and smoky atmospheres is overwhelming. The government's chief medical adviser said that working in smoky environments increases the risk of lung cancer in bar workers threefold. He added that allowing smoking in pubs which do not serve food will widen the health gap between rich and poor.*

In this case, we are using evidence from the government's chief medical adviser to support the reasoning. We can contrast this with the following passage:

> There is some controversy as to whether smoking should be banned in all public places or only some. It is not fair that some bar workers should be protected, but not others. There should be a blanket ban on smoking in public places. As the government's chief medical adviser says, it would be very negative if smoking were allowed in some public places.

In this second example, the government's chief medical adviser is appealed to as an authority, but no evidence or reasons are given. The conclusion is simply paraphrased.

Appeals to authority are often weak because a poor authority has been chosen. We need to question the expertise, relevance and credibility of the authority appealed to, using the skills learnt from Unit 1.

Appeal to popularity

An **appeal to popularity** justifies a conclusion by its popularity. For example, 'Most people are in favour of capital punishment, so the government should bring it back.' Popularity does not, however, make a measure right. It is not that popularity is a bad thing, but it is not enough to make an action right.

Appeal to tradition

An **appeal to tradition** justifies an act on the basis that it is traditional. However, the fact that something has been done for a long time does not make it right. Such arguments are often attempts to persuade us to resist change, and appealing to tradition in this way avoids the real issues. For example:

> 'We've always left weak infants on the mountainside to die. So we should carry on doing that – it's our tradition.'
> 'Our family have always donated a fifth of our income to charity. It's what we do. So we should carry on giving money to the needy.'

Exposing weak infants and giving to charity are supported in the same way here. So we should accept or reject both of them. Thus we can see that this pattern of reasoning cannot support a conclusion. If an action is wrong, a tradition of doing it cannot support its continuation.

Appeal to history

An **appeal to history** follows a similar pattern of reasoning. It suggests that because something always has happened, it will continue to happen. For example, a student might say, 'I've always passed exams without putting much effort in, so I'll breeze through my A levels too.'

However, the past is not a reliable guide to the future. The fact that something has happened before does not mean that it must happen again. All sorts of factors may intervene to produce a different result.

It is important to remember that finding an appeal to popularity, tradition, history or authority in an argument does not mean that the conclusion is wrong. What it does mean is that the conclusion cannot be supported in this way. In other words, the conclusion cannot be accepted on the basis of the reasoning given.

ACTIVITY 24

REMEMBER

You should always identify the main conclusion first.

EXAM TIP

There are two main kinds of question in the AS exam which test your understanding of flaws in an argument. In Unit 2 Section A you will find multiple choice questions which ask about flaws. In Unit 2 Section B you are likely to be asked to explain flaws in the reasoning of a longer passage.

Explain what is wrong with the reasoning in the following passages.

a) **This train is really reliable. It's due in at 6.30. It's never been late before, so I'll see you then.**

b) **There are psychological benefits to participating in the National Lottery. Knowing that they could win the jackpot gives hope to many participants who lead humdrum, boring lives. Moreover, smaller wins are quite common and, as the National Lottery organiser has said, these give a boost to those who receive them.**

c) **We should not tax aviation fuel. As the Prime Minister told senior MPs, 'You don't set out as Prime Minister or as a government to be deeply unpopular.'**

ACTIVITY 25

a) We should not disapprove of smoking in public places. It is an important part of British culture. Something particularly English would be lost with the demise of the small, smoke-fugged pub, or the aroma of Cuban cigars mingling with leather in a gentleman's club. Sanitised, open spaces scented with lavender and tinkling with Chopin will simply not have the same appeal.

Which of the following best expresses a flaw in the argument?

A   Our disapproval of smoking in public should not be affected by its status as tradition.

B   Our disapproval of smoking in public should not be affected by its popularity.

C   Just because we have always disapproved of smoking in public does not mean we always will.

D   Not all pubs will smell of lavender and play Chopin's piano music.

b) I need to get a Trendie. Trendies are the must-have items this Christmas. Everyone loves them.

Which of the following best expresses the flaw in the argument?

A   The fact that everyone loves Trendies is a good reason for you to hate them.

B   The fact that everyone loves Trendies means they are must-have items.

C   The fact that everyone loves Trendies does not mean that you need one.

D   The fact that everyone loves Trendies shows how shallow fashion is.

KEY TERMS

Two wrongs don't make a right – an attempt to justify one harmful thing on the basis of another, different, harmful thing. This is a flaw in reasoning, as one wrong action cannot justify another wrong action

Reasoning from wrong actions

Reasoning from wrong actions is a flaw committed by everyone from children through to international politicians. However, one wrong action cannot justify another wrong action. There are two subtly different forms of this flaw, the 'Two wrongs don't make a right' flaw, and the 'Tu quoque' flaw.

Two wrongs don't make a right

The **two wrongs don't make a right** flaw is an attempt to justify one bad action on the basis that another, different, bad action is accepted. It is a version of, 'Why are you telling me off for texting during the lesson? You didn't tell Jake off for spitting.' However, two wrongs don't make a right. Jake's wrong action is not a reason for you to do something wrong.

KEY TERMS

Tu quoque – an attempt to justify an action on the basis that someone else is doing it. This is a flaw in reasoning, as one wrong action cannot justify another wrong action

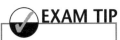

EXAM TIP

If you identify a flaw which is clearly reasoning from wrong action, you will not need to decide whether it is a Tu quoque flaw (where the actions are the same) or a Two wrongs don't make a right flaw (where the actions are different). Sometimes it is very difficult to tell if the actions are the same or different. The important thing is to say that one wrong action cannot justify another wrong action.

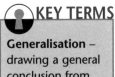

KEY TERMS

Generalisation – drawing a general conclusion from specific evidence. This is a flaw in reasoning

Tu quoque

Tu quoque is a Latin phrase which literally means 'You too'. The pattern of reasoning is that we should do something because someone else is doing it. It is a sophisticated version of 'My friends are going, why can't I?' The problem is that if it is wrong for your friends to go shoplifting in town, it is wrong for you too. Their wrong actions are not a reason for you to do something wrong as well. This applies even when politicians justify policy decisions at an international level on the basis of what other countries are doing. For example, 'Of course America should sign the Kyoto agreement to reduce greenhouse gas emissions. Other countries have.'

It may be that your friends are not doing anything wrong, or that America is entirely right not to sign the Kyoto agreement. However, our conclusions about what we do should be based on good reasons, not on what other people are doing.

Generalisation

Generalisation is drawing a general conclusion from specific evidence. The reasoning moves from one or some to all. For example, 'Jenny is a good critical thinking student. Jenny is a tall black girl. So all good critical thinking students are tall black girls.' We cannot move from Jenny to all critical thinking students. Just because one critical thinking student has a particular quality, we cannot suppose that they all do.

You may also come across a sweeping generalisation, which moves from many to all. It may well be the case that many young men are passionate about football, but this does not allow us to conclude that they all are. We cannot say that David enjoys football just because he is a young man. He may be one of the young men who does not like football. Generalisations tend to lie behind stereotypes and prejudice against certain groups of people, so it is particularly important that we recognise and combat them.

It is important not to confuse generalisation from one case with giving an example to support your reasoning. It is perfectly acceptable to make a general point and give an example to illustrate it. It is not acceptable to take a specific example and draw a general conclusion from it.

> *Not all young people are attracted by the riotous partying we associate with modern teens. Jaz prefers an environment where she can talk to her friends, and Kyle enjoys playing chess with his girlfriend more than going clubbing. We should give young people credit for being interesting and varied, instead of slamming them all for being vacuous drunks.*

Here, Jaz and Kyle are given as examples to illustrate a general point. This argument works. Compare this with the following argument:

> *Jaz prefers talking to her friends in a quiet place to going clubbing, and Kyle would rather play chess with his girlfriend. This shows that stereotypical images of young people throwing up in the gutter are rubbish.*

Here, a general conclusion is drawn from the examples of Jaz and Kyle. Two examples are not enough to debunk a stereotype.

ACTIVITY 26

Explain what is wrong with the reasoning in these arguments.

a) We cannot reduce the level of our farming subsidies from the European Common Agricultural Policy. The French are refusing to budge on their subsidies.

b) Australian researchers have shown that genetically modified peas trigger allergic reactions in mice. Genetically modified crops are simply too dangerous for human consumption.

c) We cannot afford to pay all our workers the minimum wage. We will have to use illegal immigrants to pick our strawberries as we can pay them very much less than workers protected by British law. If we look around, we can see that other farmers and the catering industry are making similar decisions.

ACTIVITY 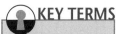27

a) Two cars were involved in the crash. One was driven by Amir Hussain, a 19-year-old male, the other by Susan Lovegood, a 49-year-old woman. As young men drive more aggressively than middle-aged women, Amir must have been to blame for the accident.

Which of the following best expresses the flaw in the argument?

A   Just because one 19-year-old man drove irresponsibly, we cannot say that they all do.

B   Just because Susan Lovegood is a woman, we cannot be sure that she drove badly.

C   Differences between men and women are too vague to be useful.

D   Just because young men tend to drive irresponsibly, we cannot be sure that Amir Hussain did.

b) Dogs and cats kept for the fur trade in China are often treated badly. They are packed into tight cages which are kicked from high lorries to the ground. However, we should not protest at this treatment. Europeans are a major market for this fur. In any case, we are prepared to keep chickens and pigs in similar conditions before we eat them.

Which of the following best expresses the flaw in the argument?

A   If we buy this fur, we are responsible for the conditions the animals are kept in.

B   The way we treat animals does not justify acceptance of the way animals are treated in China.

C   It is hypocritical for anyone who eats animals to object to the fur trade.

D   We cannot generalise from chickens in Europe to dogs in China.

KEY TERMS

Restricting the options – presenting a false and limited version of the choices available to encourage a particular course of action. This is a flaw in reasoning

Restricting the options

This flaw in reasoning is also known as a false dilemma or an 'either or' flaw. It presents a limited picture of choices available in a situation and often tries to encourage a particular course of action on the basis that there is only one, unpleasant alternative. For example, 'We must either increase the number of speed cameras on the roads, or accept increasing road deaths.' This ignores the possibilities that road deaths will not increase, or that other methods might be used to reduce road deaths.

Flaw of causation

Reasoning can be flawed if it assumes a causal connection without good reason to do so. Two common patterns such reasoning might use are:

1) *A occurs before B. So A causes B. For example, my alarm clock goes off just before the sun rises in winter. So my alarm clock beeping must cause the sun to come up.*

2) *A and B occur at the same time. So A causes B. For example, as the internet has grown, there has been a huge rise in cheating in A levels. So the internet must be the cause of the increase in cheating.*

In example 1 above, it is clear that my alarm clock beeping does not cause the sun to come up. It is a simple coincidence (co-incidence literally means 'occurring together'). In example 2, the internet is probably a means of cheating rather than a cause of it. It seems likely that cheating is caused by the pressures and possibilities of coursework.

Just because two things occur together or in quick succession, we cannot be certain that there is a causal relationship. It may simply be a correlation – a relationship between two or more things in which neither necessarily causes the other. It may be that B causes A. It may be that another factor, C, causes both A and B. We need more evidence to justify the link.

Slippery slope

A **slippery slope** flaw reasons from one possibility, through a series of events which are not properly linked, to an extreme consequence. It is called a slippery slope flaw because it is like putting one foot on a slippery slope and slithering uncontrollably to the bottom. Such reasoning is often negative. For example, 'If I don't do my homework tonight I'll fail all my exams, lose my place at university, be unemployed, get addicted to drugs and die in the gutter.' Clearly, not doing your homework *once* will not have such devastating effects. The causal links are too extreme and unjustified.

The same pattern also works with positive consequences. For example, 'If I do my homework tonight, I'll pass my exams with excellent grades, get to a good university, earn loads of money in a satisfying job and win a Nobel prize for my contributions to humanity.' Just as ignoring your homework for one night will do you little harm, so doing it just the once is unlikely to have great consequences.

ACTIVITY 28

Explain what is wrong with the reasoning in the following arguments.

a) Environmentalists plan to reintroduce wolves to fairly heavily populated parts of America and Europe, despite fears of attacks on humans. We should support this plan unless we are happy for wolves to become extinct.

b) Christmas Present Crisis! Father Christmas only has enough toys for half the good boys and girls. We must all go to Lapland and help make more toys. If we don't, our children won't get any presents. Not only that, Father Christmas will go out of business, the elves and reindeer will be unemployed, homeless and starving, we'll all have the most miserable Christmas ever and there will be an end to peace and joy.

c) The weather reporters should give us better weather. They can clearly influence the weather, as it always does what they say it will. We would like less winter in future.

ACTIVITY 29

a) Public perception of GM crops will soon improve. We have been unhappy about GM crops until now because they only benefit farmers. A major GM seed producer has recently developed a soya bean with massive health benefits for consumers. Further similar products are in production.

Which of the following best expresses the flaw in the argument?

A   It is unfair to suggest that consumers' objections to GM crops are selfish.

B   There may be other options, such as crops which benefit farmers and consumers.

C   There are too many uncertain links between one soya bean and an improvement of public opinion about GM crops.

D   The public may have other reasons for being unhappy about GM crops.

b) I have to dye my hair green today, otherwise I'll never know what it felt like to express my true personality.

Which of the following best expresses the flaw in the argument?

A   You might find that green hair does not express your true personality.

B   There may be other ways of expressing your true personality.

C   There are too many uncertain links between dyeing your hair and Inner fulfilment.

D   You may have other reasons for wanting to dye your hair green.

Circular argument

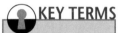
In a **circular argument** one of the reasons is the same as the conclusion, so the argument goes round in circles rather than getting anywhere. For example, 'You've got blue eyes because your eyes are blue.'

One special kind of circular reasoning is begging the question in which the reasons only work if the conclusion is true. For example, 'We know the Pope is infallible because God says so. We know that God says so because the Pope has told us, and the Pope must be right about it, because he is infallible.'

REMEMBER

If we find a flaw in an argument, it does not necessarily mean that the conclusion is wrong. We may just need to find another way of supporting the conclusion.

Confusing necessary and sufficient conditions

A necessary condition is something which has to be the case if a conclusion is to hold. Talent is a necessary condition of being a top-class sportsperson, for example.

A sufficient condition is something which is enough to support a conclusion. Committing murder is sufficient to send you to jail, for example.

Confusing necessary and sufficient conditions in an argument makes it flawed. Let's consider the following examples:

> *Jamal is really talented. He is an extremely fast runner. He's bound to run in the Olympics.*

We cannot draw the conclusion that Jamal is bound to run in the Olympics, because, although talent is necessary, it is not enough. Jamal will also need luck, determination and good training.

> *It's not as if Annie murdered anyone. She only supplied crack. So she won't go to prison.*

KEY TERMS

Attacking the arguer – attacking the person putting forward an argument rather than their argument. This is a flaw in reasoning, as an argument should be judged on its own merits

KEY TERMS

Straw person – dismissing a distorted version of an opposing argument. This is a flaw in reasoning, as it does not provide a good reason not to accept the real argument

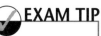

EXAM TIP

Not every attempt to answer a counter argument is flawed.

We cannot draw the conclusion that Annie will not go to prison because, although murder is sufficient to send you to prison, it is not necessary. Supplying crack will do just as well.

Attacking the arguer

An argument is flawed if it dismisses an opposite view by attacking the person putting forward that view, rather than attacking the reasoning used to support the opposing view. This kind of attack, also known as 'ad hominem' (Latin for 'against the person'), does not give us a good reason to dismiss a counter argument.

> *She's just a dizzy blonde, so of course she's talking rubbish. We can't accept her point about genetics.*

Contrary to popular misconception, the colour of someone's hair does not affect the quality of their argument.

Straw person

A **straw person** flaw builds up a distorted version of an opposing argument, in order to dismiss it. A straw person flaw often misses the point, and attacks something which does not exist. For example your school will not let the sixth form Christmas party on the premises because there are no teachers to supervise it, and there are building works going on. If you ignore these health and safety concerns, and tell everyone the teachers "don't want us to have fun" this would be misrepresenting their argument: a straw person flaw.

ACTIVITY 30

Explain what is wrong with the reasoning in the following arguments.

a) Some scientists have suggested that computer games are actually good for children. This is no doubt because scientists live in a world where social skills are a rarity and moral values are insignificant. Those of us who value the truly important things in life should continue to encourage children away from computer games.

b) Of course wizards hide from muggles. Otherwise we'd know they were there, wouldn't we?

c) Refi is bound to get the job. She has all the qualifications for it, and plenty of relevant experience.

ACTIVITY ③①

a) Photonic make up is truly beautiful. It will undoubtedly be a huge success for the cosmetic companies. The shimmering, ever-changing colours are inspired by the morpho butterfly and peacocks' tails. It is not pigments, but multiple reflections of light within the material that create the iridescent effect of this make up.

Which of the following best expresses the flaw in the argument?

    A   Although beauty may be necessary for success in cosmetics, it is not sufficient.

    B   Although beauty may be sufficient for success in cosmetics, it is not necessary.

    C   People may have other reasons for using cosmetics than increasing their beauty.

    D   Some people may find that looking like a peacock's tail does not enhance their beauty.

b) Mathilda Plume of the Tobacco Manufacturers Confederation argued that figures relating to deaths caused by smoking are distorted. She claims that health professionals count all cases of lung cancer as a smoking related disease, whether or not the person smoked. However, her vested interest renders her opinion totally unreliable, so we can be sure that the smoking death figures are accurate.

Which of the following best expresses the flaw in the argument?

    A   Mathilda Plume should not generalise from distorted statistics to the safety of smoking.

    B   Mathilda Plume's vested interest does not guarantee that her claims are wrong.

    C   Mathilda Plume's argument is shown in a false light to make it easier to dismiss.

    D   The attack on Mathilda Plume means that we cannot accept figures about smoking deaths.

SUMMARY

You should now be able to recognise the following flaws in reasoning:

- **Appeal to authority** – claiming your conclusion must be right because an expert or someone in authority supports it.

- **Appeal to popularity** – a form of argument which justifies a conclusion by its popularity.

- **Appeal to tradition** – a form of argument which supports a conclusion by saying it is traditional.

- **Appeal to history** – a form of argument which supports a conclusion by reference to history.

- **Two wrongs don't make a right** – an attempt to justify one harmful thing on the basis of another, different, harmful thing.

- **Tu quoque** – an attempt to justify an action on the basis that someone else is doing it.

- **Generalisation** – drawing a general conclusion from specific evidence.

- **Restricting the options** – presenting a false and limited version of the choices available to encourage a particular course of action.

- **Flaw of causation** – a flaw in reasoning which assumes that if two things occur together or in quick succession, one of them must cause the other.

- **Slippery slope** – reasoning from one minor event through a series of unlinked events to an extreme consequence.

- **Circular argument** – an argument that starts and ends with the same point.

- **Confusing necessary and sufficient conditions** – reasoning which confuses necessary and sufficient conditions does not support a conclusion. Something which is necessary is not always enough. Something which is enough is not always necessary.

- **Attacking the arguer** – attacking the person putting forward an argument rather than their argument.

- **Straw person** – dismissing a distorted version of an opposing argument.

In this chapter we will look at how the use of language can affect the support given to an argument. We shall also explore the status of different kinds of claim, and patterns of reasoning using principles, analogies and hypothetical claims.

Language

Language is the means by which we express our ideas. The clarity and precision with which language is used can make the difference between a strong, well supported argument and a weak one. Clumsy use of a key word can affect the strength of support given to a conclusion.

In the AS exam you may have to evaluate language use in the following ways:

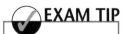

EXAM TIP

You will need to:

- *Evaluate how the use of language in an argument affects the support for the conclusion*

- *Ensure that you use language clearly and precisely when you are analysing and evaluating arguments*

- *Write with clarity and precision when you are developing your own arguments to ensure that your reasons support your conclusion precisely.*

- There may be a multiple choice question which asks you to choose the answer which best defines the meaning of a term in the context of the passage, or in an argument.

- When evaluating reasoning in section B you may be expected to identify key words used in a vague or problematic way if this affects the support given to the conclusion.

You will be expected to use clear, precise language in all your answers.

Vagueness

Vague language is not precisely focussed or clear. Words are used sloppily and with vague reference. Some candidates in Critical Thinking exams fail to gain marks because their answers are too vague or sloppy for the examiner to be sure what they mean.

If the conclusion of an argument is, 'We should encourage the trend of young people choosing not to use cosmetics' (OCR, June 2005, Paper 2, Q 3), the following answers would be too vague to gain marks:

> *They shouldn't use it.*
> *It should be banned.*
> *Cosmetics is [sic] bad.*
> *Young people shouldn't use cosmetics.*

Some of these answers are better than others, but even the last one, which is better than the others, does not capture the essential idea that young people are choosing not to use cosmetics, and this trend should be encouraged. It implies that young people are being told what not to do, which is far stronger than the actual conclusion.

It is more important to be clear and precise than artistic and flowing in your use of language. Read the following question and the four student answers:

> *Identify and explain a flaw in the following passage:*
>
> *'Travellers have been evicted from the local DIY superstore car park this week. One campaigner suggested that sites should be maintained around the country for use by travellers, but we should not listen to such wishy washy liberal bleating. These New Age hippies are happy to enjoy the benefits of our society. So these travellers should accept our way of life.'*
>
> *Answer A: The author attacks the arguer rather than the argument, discounting the campaigner's arguments without examining what they say.*
>
> *Answer B: The author expresses an unfair and reprehensible prejudice against the travelling community. Liberal principles are a vital part of a civilised society and should not be condemned.*
>
> *Answer C: The author uses words such as 'wishy washy' which are not good English, and uses evocative words such as 'bleating' to make us feel that the campaigner is not very intelligent.*
>
> *Answer D: The author uses the words 'travellers' and 'New Age hippies' as if they were the same. However, they are not precisely the same, so it does not make sense to draw a conclusion about travellers from reasoning about one small group of travellers.*

Answer A is plain and simple, but it attracts marks because it is correct. Answer B may be written in perfect and elegant English, but it does not attract marks because it does not address the flaw in the pattern of the reasoning. Answer C assesses the quality of English in an argument, which does not gain marks. Answer D attracts marks because it makes a point about the vague use of a key word, and how this affects support for the conclusion.

Many words have more than one meaning, or a range of meanings and connotations. It is important to be clear how a word is being used in a particular argument and to be precise about its meaning, because this can affect the argument. In Critical Thinking, we are particularly concerned about vague use of language if it means that the words or ideas do not give precise support to the conclusion.

> The town centre is an ugly mess of sixties concrete blocks with dull shops, nothing to do and a problem with binge drinking and violence. We would like to improve the town centre. The council intends to improve the town centre. So, because we all want improvement, we should support the council.

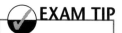

KEY TERMS

Ambiguous – a word is ambiguous if it can have more than one meaning and it is not clear which meaning is intended in a particular context

EXAM TIP

Using language vaguely is one of the best ways of ensuring that you gain very few marks in a Critical Thinking exam. Every time you write words such as 'it' or 'they', consider what you really mean. What is 'it'? Or 'they'?

In this argument, we need to be sure that we all have the same understanding of improvement. Improvement is a vague term. It might mean any of the following: razing to the ground; making more economic; making more attractive; making a dramatic statement; providing more entertainment; providing more variety; increasing policing; making safer. We should support the council only if their idea of improvement agrees with ours.

One special form of vagueness is ambiguity. A word or phrase is **ambiguous** if it can have more than one meaning and it is not clear which meaning is intended in a particular context. For example, 'If your child does not like runny cream, whip it.' The vague use of language means that 'it' could apply to either the child or the cream.

In the town centre example above, the word 'improvement' is ambiguous because we cannot be sure how it is being used in this context. So we cannot be sure that we should support the council.

A further form of vagueness is inconsistency. A word or phrase is used inconsistently if it has more than one meaning, and is used with different meanings during an argument. For example:

> The town centre is an ugly mess of sixties concrete blocks with dull shops, nothing to do and a problem with binge drinking and violence. We, the residents, believe that it should be improved. We propose more police on Friday and Saturday nights, safe venues for young people to gather and the demolition of the Bicorn building. The council also proposes improvement. It wants to encourage investment in new buildings, shops and industry. So, as we all want improvement, we should support the council.

Here, it is spelled out what improvement means, and in each case it means something different. The use of 'improvement' here is inconsistent. The overall effect is weak support for the conclusion, as the word is being used in two different ways.

ACTIVITY 32

Conviction rates vary between police forces. In Bedfordshire only 51% of cases end in a conviction, whereas in Warwickshire the figure is 93%. So there are victims in Bedfordshire who have been deprived of justice.

a) Which of the following best expresses the meaning of justice as used in this context?

  A   Dealing fairly and impartially with offenders.

  B   Ensuring that the punishment fits the crime.

  C   Infliction of punishment on an offender.

  D   The administration of legal proceedings.

b) Discuss any problems raised by the use of justice in this way.

KEY TERMS

Conflation – bringing two or more different concepts together and treating them as the same thing

Conflation

Conflation is bringing two or more different concepts together and treating them as the same thing. For example:

> Obesity is a growing problem in western societies. The increasing number of people who lead a sedentary lifestyle is causing tremendous problems for health provision and insurance. If we want to avoid an obesity crisis we must encourage these people to get fit.

In this short argument, it is assumed that obese and unfit are the same – that is, they are conflated. Although many obese people are unfit, a significant minority are fat but fit. Conversely, many thin people are not fit. This conflation causes problems for the argument. If it is unfitness which causes healthcare problems, it is unfitness which should be addressed, and the target audience needs to be expanded beyond the obese.

Conflation is sometimes treated as a flaw in reasoning in Critical Thinking mark schemes. It is certainly a serious weakness, because it often means we cannot accept a conclusion on the basis of the reasoning given. Strictly speaking, the weakness comes from the poor use of language rather than the pattern of reasoning. If you are asked to evaluate a passage, you would gain marks for pointing out that vague use of a key term, or conflation of key terms, weakens the support for the conclusion.

ACTIVITY 33

Evaluate the use of language in this argument:

'Northern Universities XI cricket team defeated Lancashire on Saturday – a surprising result, as you would not have expected a group of pen-pushers to be so skillful with the willow.'

KEY TERMS

Claim – something which is stated, or claimed to be the case

Claims

Any part of an argument can be referred to as a **claim**. A claim is something which is stated, or claimed to be the case – it may be a fact or opinion, a principle or a hypothetical claim. The word claim suggests to us that we should suspend belief in its truth until the claim is verified or supported with reasons. This is important in Critical Thinking because we are mostly interested in how an argument works if we assume its claims to be true.

Fact and opinion

A fact is information which can be verified and which is held to be true. Factual claims in an argument, therefore, consist of information which can be verified. We treat them as true, but our acceptance of their truth is suspended until we can check the facts.

Opinion cannot be verified. For example, 'Peas are the most revolting vegetable' cannot be true or false in the same way that 'Peas are small, round and green' can. We present this belief as a fact, but someone who thinks peas are delicious is not wrong.

It is tempting to believe that an objective argument should be restricted to factual claims. However, subjective opinion can have a role in objective argument. For example:

R1 (opinion)	Cigarette smoke smells disgusting and I hate the way it lingers on my clothes and hair.
R2 (verifiable factual claim)	I am also asthmatic.
C (recommendation)	So I should avoid smoky pubs.

Here R1, which is an opinion, is just as strong a reason to support the conclusion as the factual claim, R2.

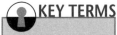

KEY TERMS

Principle – a statement which applies to a wide range of situations, rather like a rule. A principle can act as a reason, intermediate conclusion, assumption or conclusion in an argument

Principles

Principles, sometimes called general principles, are rule-like statements which apply beyond the immediate circumstances of an argument. They tend to be a guide to action. If we say, 'You should have brushed your hair before coming to college this morning,' we are commenting on a specific case. If, however, we say, 'You should brush your hair before going to college in the morning,' we are using a principle which applies beyond a particular morning.

Many principles are moral guidelines and have to do with right and wrong, with what is fair or with how best to live our lives, such as, 'You should give to charity' or 'It is unfair to make war on a country which has not been aggressive.' Others deal with more practical matters, such as, 'Schools should balance their budgets' or 'You should stop eating when you are full.' Most are recommendations. They are not verifiable and are thus different from factual statements. 'We must protect the environment' is a different type of statement from 'There are 22 birds sitting on the roof' or 'Climate change threatens to destroy our world.'

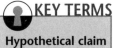

KEY TERMS

Hypothetical claim – an 'if … then' statement used in hypothetical reasoning

Hypothetical claims

A **hypothetical claim** is an 'if … then' statement used in hypothetical reasoning.

In Unit 1 you looked at suppositional reasoning, which is one form of hypothetical reasoning. You learned how to form hypothetical claims about the credibility of sources, documents, participants and claims. For example, instead of making a weak claim, 'As far as we know, X is neutral, so their claims are likely to be credible,' you were encouraged to write a hypothetical claim: 'If X is not a friend or enemy of Y, X is neutral, which would make their claims credible.' This helped you to focus on the specific things we would want to know and check about X.

As we have also discussed in Chapter 4 of this book, questioning what you need to know or check about evidence is an important skill in evaluating evidence. In both cases, you start with the conclusion you want, and test the conditions (the 'ifs) that might support or weaken that conclusion.

In this chapter, we are concerned with hypothetical claims and hypothetical reasoning which starts with a condition (an 'if') and explores what might happen. This is the other way around to the sort of thinking we are doing when we test evidence. Hypothetical claims predict what will happen if ..., for example: 'If we don't keep hospitals clean, more people will catch nasty bugs like MRSA and die.'

Some statements look similar to hypothetical claims, but are not, for example, 'I want a winter suntan even if I get skin cancer from the sunbed.' This is not a hypothetical claim: it is a statement about what I want. However, 'If you use a sunbed too often, you may get skin cancer' is a hypothetical claim, because it makes a prediction. It does not matter whether there is a proven causal link between the condition and the consequence. It is the 'if ... then' form of the statement, and its status as a prediction, which makes it hypothetical.

It is difficult to verify hypothetical claims without testing them. In some circumstances we can test such a claim. 'If you drop lithium into water it will fizz', can be tested by dropping lithium into water to see what happens. However, some claims cannot be tested for practical or moral reasons. 'If we keep teenage boys in a box until they are 20, they will come out much nicer at the end.' Sadly, we'll never know!

ACTIVITY 34

Identify the different kinds of claim:

a) Doctors should save life, not take it.

b) Sailing is the best way to spend a sunny, breezy day.

c) If you want to get to France, you should use the Chunnel.

d) Phil's laptop cost £534.

e) My teacher is rubbish.

Reasoning

In previous chapters, we have concentrated on analysing and evaluating reasoning which has consisted largely of factual claims and opinions. We will now consider some of the special issues involved in evaluating principles, hypothetical reasoning and one further pattern of reasoning – the use of analogy to support a conclusion.

Application of principles

In a Critical Thinking exam you may have to:

- identify a general principle in an argument
- think of another principle that isn't in the passage but which would be relevant
- find another situation in which the principle applies
- think of an exception where the principle does not apply
- decide whether the government or an individual should act on a particular principle
- evaluate whether the principle really supports the conclusion which has been drawn.

> I am in a sweetshop and there is no one watching me. I could easily take some sweets. But we should not steal, so I will buy some when the shopkeeper comes back.

In this example the principle is, 'We should not steal.' We can think of many other situations in which this principle applies. Taking your friend's mobile, or even using it to make an hour-long call to Australia and not mentioning it, would be stealing, and therefore something we should not do. We can justify this by using more principles:

R1	Stealing hurts someone else
R2 (principle)	We should avoid hurting other people.
R3 (principle)	It is not fair for someone else to pay for or suffer for the things that you want.
C	So, we should not steal.

Can we say that there is an exception to the principle? If the person we are taking things from is so rich that it won't hurt them, can we justify stealing from them? Not really, because the second principle we used, that it is not fair for them to pay for things you want, still applies.

But what if they are rich, and won't notice, and my family will die if I don't steal food for them? Well, this is a different situation from stealing someone's car because you're bored and want some excitement. It is certainly unfair that some people have so much while others have so little. But this does not necessarily make it acceptable to steal from them. You may like to discuss this in class. Remember, the fact that we can find exceptions does not mean that the principle is not generally valid.

ACTIVITY 35

Work in groups. Think of situations in which the following principles apply, and in which they do not.

a) Killing can never be justified.

b) We should provide aid to those who need it.

c) A right always brings a duty with it.

d) Children should be seen and not heard.

e) People who do not contribute to society should not benefit from it.

ACTIVITY

Identify the principles in the following arguments.

a) Our lifestyle is not sustainable. We are destroying our world with our emissions, our rubbish and our exploitation of natural resources. We should put the future of the world before our selfish desires. This means we should moderate our lifestyle.

b) We should all become vegetarians. Animals feel pain and we should not hurt them. Farming and killing them involves hurting them.

c) Every year thousands of people inflict damage on themselves. It is not fair that genuinely ill people have to wait for treatment, so people who cause their own problems should not be treated on the NHS.

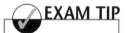 **KEY TERMS**

Analogy – a form of argument which uses parallel situations to encourage the audience to accept a conclusion

Analogies

Analogies are a form of argument which uses parallel situations to encourage the audience to accept a conclusion. Analogies suggest that two situations are significantly parallel, that is, they work in the same way. So, if we accept a conclusion about one situation, because the two work in the same way, we should accept it about the other.

> It is unfair to keep teenagers in school. It deprives them of freedom, self-esteem and purpose in life. We may as well send them straight to prison and have done with it.

This example claims that confining teenagers in school works in a significantly similar way to putting them in prison. As we would certainly think it unfair to put all teenagers in prison, and the two situations are said to be parallel, we should also accept the conclusion that it is unfair to keep teenagers in school.

EXAM TIP

Do not assume that every comparison in an argument is an analogy. You will not impress the examiner if you describe a bad comparison as a 'false analogy'.

Analogy is a special form of comparison. It compares whole situations and claims that we should reason about them in the same way. One significant difference weakens an analogy, as we shall discuss later. A normal comparison highlights one or more points of similarity, but does not claim that the two situations are parallel. It allows for significant difference and there is no requirement that patterns of reasoning be shared.

Saying 'Zara is like a cat that's got the cream' is a comparison, but not an analogy. It is not implied that Zara has fur and whiskers, or that she is cat-like in any other way, simply that she is smug because she has got something she wanted (and which may not have been allowed).

ACTIVITY 37

Do the following arguments use analogies or comparisons?

a) A child dies every 15 seconds from unsafe water. It's like 15 jumbo jets full of children crashing every day. This situation is not acceptable.

b) We should use all the means at our disposal to rid our society of drug dealers and terrorists. When cancerous cells develop in the body we surgically remove them or kill them with drugs and radiotherapy before they can spread into healthy areas. We accept that some healthy cells will be destroyed along with the sick ones, but so long as the whole body survives this is not a problem.

c) Her mind is like a well-ordered filing cabinet – drawer after drawer of memories and ideas organised logically and coherently.

Evaluating analogy

Analogies should create a parallel between one situation and a familiar situation to make it easier to follow a pattern of thought, or create a clear image in our mind to make it easier to follow abstract reasoning. Two situations are being compared very strongly, such that anything we accept about one situation, we must also accept about the other.

When evaluating an analogy, we should first be clear what the situations being compared are. For example:

> *We cannot expect politicians to be honest in the run up to a general election. We may as well leave a child alone in a sweet shop.*

In this analogy, it is not politicians and children in general which are supposed to be similar. It is the situation of facing temptation with great reward and little possibility of being caught and punished.

The second step in evaluating an analogy is to consider significant similarities and differences between the two situations. Let's take the example about politicians and children in a sweet shop:

- *Similarities:* Someone standing before great temptation with much to gain, expecting not to be caught. Both are thrown upon their conscience and understanding of right and wrong.
- *Differences:* Children have a developing sense of conscience and still need to learn. Politicians are grown adults and ought to be able to act on an understanding of right and wrong.

The third step is to decide whether the differences between the situations are significant, and whether they outweigh the similarities. One important difference can make an analogy weak, even if there are many similarities. In the case of the politicians, the fact that politicians are adults who should be able to act on an understanding of right and wrong is a significant difference. The analogy may show us why politicians are tempted, but it does not support the claim, 'We cannot expect politicians to be honest in the run up to a general election.'

Let's work through another example.

> There are many advocates of banning boxing on the grounds that participants may sustain serious injury. This is like saying we should ban motor sport because drivers may be hurt in a crash. However, both sports have strict rules to ensure safety, and participants know the risks. So, we should sit back and enjoy the skill of these brave men.

Step 1: Identify the precise situations being compared

The risk of injury to boxers is said to be similar to the risk of injury to drivers in motor sport.

Step 2: Identify significant similarities and differences

○ Similarities: Both sports involve a significant risk of injury. Both (as stated) enforce safety regulations.

○ Differences: In boxing the aim of the sport is to injure each other. In motor sport injury is an unfortunate side effect of unplanned crashes.

Step 3: Evaluate whether the differences outweigh the similarities, and whether the analogy helps support the conclusion

To me, it seems that the intentional nature of the injuries caused in boxing is a significant difference which weakens the analogy.

ACTIVITY 38

Evaluate the analogies in the following arguments.

a) It has been suggested that darts should be an olympic sport. This proposal should not be taken seriously. Darts involves no physical exertion at all. We may as well introduce competitive reading as an olympic sport.

b) There is no scientific controversy between intelligent design and evolution. The case for teaching them as valid alternatives is no stronger than the case for teaching students about some supposed controversy between astrology and astronomy.

Source: New Scientist, *editorial, 9 July 2005 p. 5*

c) We need greater research into GM crops before deciding whether to allow their use in Britain. However, the very process of research involves growing and eating them and evaluating how much damage they do. It is like setting off a nuclear bomb to see what happens. By the time we know what happens, it will be too late to undo the damage.

Hypothetical reasoning

As we discussed earlier, a hypothetical claim considers 'what if …?' It looks at the consequences that might occur if something were the case. This can help us to make decisions about how to act, depending upon what happens. Hypothetical reasoning uses a hypothetical claim as a reason to support a conclusion.

> *If it rains, we will get wet. The children don't like getting wet, so we should stay at home.*

We cannot conclude that we will definitely get wet, because we do not know whether it will rain. The rain is a hypothetical, uncertain event – an unfulfilled condition. But we can predict logical consequences and consider what will or would happen if it did rain. We can make plans for the future on the basis of this reasoning – we can take a raincoat with us or stay at home.

When we are evaluating hypothetical reasoning, we need to consider the following:

- Is the hypothetical claim as a whole true?
- Is the hypothetical event likely?
- Are the hypothetical consequences likely?

We need to consider the truth of the hypothetical statement as a whole, rather than the individual parts of it. Some hypothetical statements are clearly true as a whole, even if their parts are not. We will get wet if it rains, and the truth of this does not depend on whether it is raining now.

On the other hand, we must not let the truth of a hypothetical claim lull us into forgetting that the parts are not necessarily factually true at the moment. We need to consider how likely the condition (the 'if') is. Just because we will get wet if it rains, this is not a good reason to stay at home on a sunny summer's day.

Look at the following example:

> If I get the job, I'll have twice as much money, so I'll be able to buy a Maserati. I'll pop to the show room.

In this example, I need to remember that I haven't yet got the job. It may be true that I'll be able to buy a flash car if I do get it, but I would be unwise to rush out and buy one now. We must not treat the unfulfilled condition of getting the job as hard fact.

Some hypothetical claims are less evidently true or certain. We cannot be sure what will happen to those poor teenage boys in a box. This affects our evaluation of reasoning which relies on that claim. In cases like this where we cannot test a hypothetical claim for ethical or practical reasons, we need to make judgements about the likelihood of the suggested consequences using existing evidence and our understanding of logic.

> If you have unprotected sex, you will get a sexually transmitted infection and she will have a baby. So you should use a condom.

In this case, the consequences highlighted in the hypothetical claim are too strong. Unprotected sex can lead to sexually transmitted infections and pregnancy, but it is not a certainty, in the same way as getting wet in the rain. However, the risk is great enough that we cannot challenge the conclusion.

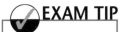
EXAM TIP

In the exam, you are likely to be asked to identify hypothetical reasoning. If you are asked to evaluate it, consider:

- Is the hypothetical claim as a whole true?
- Is the hypothetical event likely?
- Are the hypothetical consequences likely?

ACTIVITY ❸❾

REMEMBER

Remember to avoid slippery slope flaws.

Consider the possible consequences of the following hypothetical events. Discuss in groups how likely these consequences are.

1) **If the government detains terrorist suspects without trial …**

2) **If Britain leaves the European Union …**

3) **If we spend December in New Zealand …**

4) **If I try crack cocaine just once …**

ACTIVITY ❹❿

Identify and evaluate any principles, analogies and hypothetical reasoning in the following passage:

For too long, Africa has scarred the conscience of the world. In order to aid poorer nations, we must focus on developing their own skills base.

African nations need to provide their own solutions to African problems. So Africa needs help to develop its own capacity in science, engineering, medicine and technology. Most research is carried out in developed countries and focuses on their own interests. Just 10% of the global budget for health research is spent on the diseases that affect 90% of the world's population. If Africa had its own science and technology base, this balance would be redressed.

If Africa can develop centres of excellence in science and technology, it will be able to close the scientific gap with the rest of the world. It will be able to provide a skills base right across the educational system. From this will come the capacity to provide, for example, clean water and hygienic living conditions. Basic services like this are desperately needed.

We do not encourage mature, independent adults by continuing to spoon feed them beyond babyhood. Neither will we encourage the poorest countries in the world to develop to maturity unless we allow them access to the spoon. Aid for developing nations must focus on the development of science and technology.

SUMMARY

You should now be able to:

- Identify key words which are used vaguely and weaken the support given to a conclusion
- Identify a range of types of claim, including factual statements, opinions, principles and hypothetical claims
- Identify and evaluate reasoning using principles and hypothetical claims
- Identify and evaluate reasoning using analogy to support a conclusion.

Developing your own arguments

7

So far, this book has been concerned with looking at other people's arguments and developing the strategies needed to analyse and evaluate them. There will now be a change of focus as we introduce some ideas and approaches (and pitfalls) in writing your own arguments. This is a skill that attracts a significant amount of marks in the exam.

Developing your own arguments is an important critical thinking skill. A key point to remember is that you cannot 'win' an argument by merely criticising others. You also have to be able to put forward your own case in a reasoned and disciplined way.

The process of writing your own arguments

The following sections will outline strategies that you can use to make sure that your arguments are both persuasive and well-structured.

Clearly stating the conclusion

The first step in forming your own argument is being clear about the conclusion that you are heading for. That may sound obvious, but you might be surprised by the number of students who forget to write down their conclusion. Make sure that your own arguments always contain a clearly stated conclusion. You may find it helpful if you put the conclusion either first or last. For instance:

> C   *Cats are excellent pets.*
> R1 *They are affectionate.*
> R2 *They are full of fun.*
> R3 *They do not take too much looking after.*
>
> *or*
>
> R1 *Cats are affectionate.*
> R2 *They are full of fun.*
> R3 *They do not take too much looking after.*
> C   *Therefore, cats are excellent pets.*

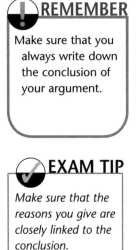

REMEMBER

Make sure that you always write down the conclusion of your argument.

EXAM TIP

Make sure that the reasons you give are closely linked to the conclusion.

It is not wrong to put the conclusion in other places in your argument, but it is often clearer if it is at the beginning or end. Many students find it easiest to put the conclusion at the end of their arguments.

Keeping a close link between reasons and conclusions

The second step in forming your own argument is to think of some reasons that support the conclusion. Strong, persuasive arguments contain reasons that give good support to the conclusion. To put it another way, in strong arguments there is a close link between the reasons and the conclusion. Thinking of reasons that give good support to the conclusion is vital to forming a strong argument.

We can illustrate this by showing some arguments where the reasons do give strong support to the conclusion and others where the reasons do not support the conclusion so well. Imagine that you are trying to argue that digital cameras are better than conventional film cameras.

> *Digital cameras are smaller than film cameras. Therefore digital cameras are better.*

As it stands, the reason gives very little support to the conclusion, because size may or may not be related to the issue of whether the digital camera is better. If we accept the idea that the size of the camera is related to the relative merits of the two cameras, we need to do something with the argument to show this. So we can improve the argument by including a second reason:

> *Digital cameras are smaller than film cameras. Size is a key factor in choosing a camera. Therefore digital cameras are better.*

This is better than our first version, but it is still not very persuasive as it seems unlikely that size *alone* would make a digital camera *better*, given the many things that cameras do.

We can make a closer link between the reason and the conclusion by making sure that the argument addresses the important things

! REMEMBER

When two reasons support a conclusion jointly, both are needed to give the conclusion support. When two reasons support a conclusion independently, either on its own would support the conclusion.

✓ EXAM TIP

Make sure that you include at least two reasons in the arguments that you write in exams.

that cameras do. After all, if a camera is better, it must be *better* at something related to the things that cameras do. For instance:

> *Taking pictures with a digital camera is easier than with a film camera. The picture quality of digital cameras is equal to that of film cameras. Therefore digital cameras are better.*

The argument establishes that digital cameras are easier to use *and* that the picture quality is similar. Taken together (the reasons jointly support the conclusion), this gives us good reason to believe that digital cameras are, in fact, better than film cameras.

Including a third reason about digital cameras – that they are more flexible to use – would give even more support to our conclusion.

Include several reasons in your argument

The arguments that we have used demonstrate that a strong, coherent argument will have several reasons to support the conclusion. When you are writing an argument, you will need to think of several reasons that develop your idea and give good support to your conclusion. In the exam, you will specifically be asked to write arguments that contain several reasons. There is no target number, but there must be *at least* two or three to make a strong argument.

ACTIVITY 41

Write at least two reasons that would support each of the following conclusions:

a) You should buy me a drink.

b) You should give me a pay rise.

c) My mobile phone is one of the best on the market.

d) Teaching is a very good career.

Do your reasons jointly support the conclusion or independently support the conclusion?

Strong and weak conclusions

Another way that a close link can be made between reasons and conclusion is to make the conclusion 'weaker'. By this we mean make it a little less specific or less definite. Consider the following two versions:

> a) *Everyone wanting to buy a new car should buy an estate car rather than a hatchback.*
>
> b) *Everyone wanting to buy a new car should consider the advantages that estate cars have over hatchbacks.*

KEY TERMS

Strong conclusion – a conclusion that is very specific and tightly defined

Weak conclusion – a conclusion that is not so specific or tightly defined

The first one is a very strong conclusion because the outcome it suggests is very specific and would apply in all situations. We would have a very hard job to successfully argue that *everyone* should buy an estate car. However, we are more likely to be successful in arguing that everyone should at least consider the advantages of an estate car, without suggesting that they go on to buy one. The second conclusion is therefore weaker, as it suggests a less tightly defined outcome.

We will finish this section by considering a very poor argument where the conclusion is not supported by the reasons because it is far too strong.

> R Drinking too much coffee may lead to headaches.
> R Drinking too much coffee may lead to disturbed sleep.
> C Coffee should be banned.

The two reasons given suggest that there are problems with drinking coffee, which might lead us to think that we need to take some action. The conclusion given goes much further than that and suggests the most extreme action. The conclusion is far too strong. It would be better to give a *weaker* conclusion in order to make a *stronger* argument. Concluding that we should cut down our intake of coffee would be a much more reasonable conclusion from the reasons given.

ACTIVITY 42

Explain whether the following are strong or weak conclusions:

a) Clam shell mobile phones are much better than other types of phone.

b) Moving to a bungalow might have advantages for an elderly person.

c) Reducing the amount of fat in our diet is part of a healthy approach to eating.

d) Reducing the amount of fat in our diet prevents heart disease.

Structured arguments

The previous section showed us that we need to think of several reasons to make an argument persuasive. We now need to consider how to structure the argument to ensure that various parts of the argument work well together.

Writing a long list of reasons will certainly make an argument, but it is generally considered to be a very simple way of arguing:

> *Smoking causes lung cancer. Smoking creates unpleasant smells. Smoking causes heart disease. Smoking creates a nuisance for non-smokers. Smoking is very expensive. Therefore you should stop smoking.*

It is not that this approach is wrong, but it does not resemble the more sophisticated and persuasive arguments that we are trying to write. The following sections will show you how to write a more developed and well-structured argument.

Including an intermediate conclusion

The first step in writing a well-structured argument is to make sure that it contains an intermediate conclusion, drawn along the way to the main conclusion. We can re-work the above argument about the dangers of smoking, beginning as follows:

> R   *Smoking causes lung cancer.*
> R   *Smoking causes heart disease.*
> IC   *Therefore, smoking is likely to lead to premature death.*

This first part of the argument ends with the intermediate conclusion.

The great thing about establishing an intermediate conclusion is that it then gives you many more choices about how to continue

the argument – it allows you to go on to *develop* your argument. So far we have established that the dangers of smoking are likely to lead to a premature death. Most of us would consider this a bad thing. We might continue the argument:

> R   Smoking causes lung cancer.
> R   Smoking causes heart disease.
> IC   Therefore, smoking is likely to lead to premature death.
> R   Everybody wants to live longer.
> C   Therefore, you should give up smoking.

This is not perfect, but we now have a structured argument that we can work with. The structure is:

$$R + R \rightarrow IC + R \rightarrow C$$

This is a very useful structure to use as a starting point for writing your own arguments. It is a relatively simple structure that contains all the vital elements. It can be used as a base from which to form more complex, sophisticated arguments.

Here is another argument about digital cameras that fits this structure:

> R   Digital cameras do not require different types of film for different lighting conditions.
> R   Poor pictures can be easily deleted from a digital camera and do not have to be developed.
> IC   Therefore, digital cameras are more practical to use.
> R   They are also smaller than film cameras.
> C   Therefore, digital cameras are better.

It is important to note that this is a suggested argument structure. It is not the only one or the best one. However, it is useful to have a simple structure in mind when beginning to practise the skill of writing your own arguments.

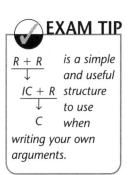

!REMEMBER

A structured argument will always contain several reasons and an intermediate conclusion.

✓EXAM TIP

$\frac{R + R}{\downarrow}$ is a simple and useful
$\frac{IC + R}{\downarrow}$ structure to use
C when
writing your own arguments.

ACTIVITY 43

Write structured arguments, following the above pattern, for these conclusions:

a) **Cats are better pets than dogs.**

b) **We should consider banning the sport of fishing.**

c) **Newly qualified drivers should not be allowed to drive on motorways.**

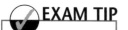

EXAM TIP

Exam questions will ask you to challenge or support the conclusion of a passage. Starting with a counter reason can help focus your mind on where you want to go with the argument, because you know that you will begin by challenging the counter reason in some way.

As a further example, suppose that you have read a passage that suggests that hamsters are the best pets for a younger child, because they are so easy to look after. You might argue against this as follows:

CA	Although hamsters are very easy to look after
R	They offer little interest for a younger child, as they are only active at night time
R	They also do not really like to be handled
IC	Therefore, a younger child is unlikely to enjoy owning a hamster
R	There are several other small animals that are easy to look after and are more entertaining
Ex	Such as rabbits and guinea pigs
C	Therefore, hamsters are not the best pets for a younger child

ACTIVITY 45

Argue against each of the following:

a) **There are very high costs involved in staging the Olympics. A lot of cities are still in debt many years after the games and it is therefore to be regretted that London won the 2012 games.**

b) **The legal age for driving should be raised to 18. After all, we are not allowed to vote until 18. These are both very responsible acts and the age limit should be the same for both.**

Writing your own arguments in the exam

In the time available to you in an exam it is unlikely that you will be able to write an argument, evaluate it and then make major changes. The best approach is to have a few simple guidelines in mind as you think of the argument so that you do not need to make too many changes later on. The section headings of this chapter could usefully form a checklist:

- Make sure that you have a clearly stated conclusion.
- Make sure that you have several reasons that do support the intermediate or main conclusion.
- Make sure that you do have an intermediate conclusion.
- Make sure that you have a clear structure.

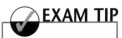

In addition, you should also try to ensure that your arguments do not rely on too many assumptions (see Chapter 2) and do not contain too many of the flaws that we covered in Chapter 5.

To help with writing your own arguments, you may find it useful to look at an argument written by someone who has *not* followed the guidelines above. Suggestions for improving it are given at the end of the discussion.

> **Your letters**
>
> Football is a fantastic game. Crowds go wild when a goal is scored, showing what an exciting game it is. When the national team play, everyone is glued to the television, willing them to win. Some killjoys talk about the violence at matches, but there were no arrests at any of the premiership matches last weekend.
>
> *Tara, Sunderland*

The first sentence is the main conclusion – football is a fantastic game. However, it is not clear how some of the reasons given support this conclusion. The lack of violence does not really affect the game's interest or excitement. Support for the national team does nothing to show the qualities of the game itself (but may support another conclusion about the importance of national teams). The excitement described would support the conclusion, as long as we assume that most games involve goals, which is not always the case.

Equally, it is clear that not 'everyone' is glued to the television – this is overstating the case. 'Everyone' is often used on news or sports broadcasts when they really mean 'a lot of people'. This sort of sloppiness has no place in critical thinking arguments.

The argument seems to want us to assume (or generalise) that because there was no violence last weekend, there is in general little violence at football matches. However, there is nothing to suggest that this is the case, and we cannot rely on this assumption/generalisation. Finally, there is no obvious structure to the argument, or intermediate conclusion present.

Now that we know what is wrong with this argument, what could we do to improve it? The most important way would be to include reasons that more closely support the conclusion. These reasons need to be connected to the game itself. Perhaps:

R   Football is a fast paced, skillful game.
Or
R   Football can be played and enjoyed by all ages and all skill levels.

We can also remove some obvious problems from the original. Rather than using 'everyone' we could say that a 'significant number' of people enjoy watching the national team.

The last sentence could be improved by including a more general comment about decreases in violence that would offer more support to the conclusion than selecting just one weekend:

R   Some will say that it is not a fantastic game because of the violence at big matches, but evidence shows that violence at matches has reduced considerably over recent seasons.

Fitting in an intermediate conclusion would also help. We could have something like:

R   Crowds go wild when a goal is scored.
R   Goals are scored in the vast majority of games.
IC   Football is a very exciting game.

Combining this intermediate conclusion with the two reasons given about the game itself would give much better support to the final conclusion. As a result, we now have a more persuasive argument that would receive a higher mark in the exam than the original version.

ACTIVITY 46

Write an argument to persuade someone that a sport (or pastime) that you enjoy is fantastic.

SUMMARY

At the end of this chapter, you should:

- Appreciate that writing your own arguments is just as important as criticising others

- Understand the importance of clearly stating the conclusion of your argument

- Be able to include several reasons to support your chosen conclusion

- Be able to include an intermediate conclusion as part of writing a more developed argument

- Be able to work to some common argument structures

- Know how to include evidence and examples in your arguments

- Use the strategies outlined in this chapter as a method of planning your own arguments before you write them down.

Preparing for the exam

8

Chapters 1 to 7 have introduced the important skills that you will need to answer the exam questions in Unit 2. This final chapter will describe some strategies that you can use as you apply these skills to the exam questions, as well as giving a broad outline of the structure of the exam.

Before the exam

Critical Thinking is a skills-based subject without a large body of knowledge that needs to be committed to memory. There isn't, therefore, a large amount of information that you need to memorise before the exam, although a familiarity with the key terms used in this book will be most helpful. You should also read through the glossary published by the OCR exam board.

This does not mean that there is nothing to do before the exam. Like all skills, practice is essential to perform at a high level. Working through the exercises in this book or those given to you by your teacher will help you prepare for the exam. Your teacher may also give you past papers to practise on.

The exam

The Unit 2 exam lasts for 1 hour and 45 minutes and is split into three distinct sections:

Section A   20 multiple choice questions
Section B   A series of questions that require you to analyse and evaluate material given in a number of stimulus documents
Section C   A chance to show your skills in writing your own arguments.

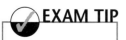

EXAM TIP

It is essential that you use the time available wisely. The total marks available are distributed over all three sections and it is important not to spend too long on any one question. Guidance is given on the front of the paper. Working at a steady rate throughout the paper is the best strategy.

Section A

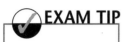

The multiple choice questions consist of a short passage followed by a question and four potential answers, only one of which is correct. Some questions will be more demanding than others. You will record your answers with a pencil on a mark sheet. It is vital that you do not spend more than 40 minutes on the multiple choice questions. This means no more than 2 minutes per question.

With limited time available, it is helpful to have strategies that focus your effort. Here are some suggestions:

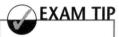

- Do not be tempted to read the answers before you have read the passage. Although this might seem helpful, it can lead to missing important words in the passage because you are already focussed on the wording of the answers. However, it is often helpful to read the question before reading the passage.

- Read carefully and accurately. Often a single word can be very important to the meaning of a reason or argument.

- Try to identify the structure of the argument presented in the passage as you read it. Look out for indicator words.

- Identify the conclusion of the passage as you read it Some questions will ask you to identify an expression of the main conclusion. The question refers to an expression of the conclusion because the wording given in the answers will not be exactly the same as in the passage. It is therefore important to be sure of the wording in the passage before reading the different versions in the potential answers.

- Try not to get 'stuck' on a particular question. Time is short and it may be better to go with your first thought rather than spend too much time puzzling over one question.

- Remember that some passages will not have a conclusion. Some questions will ask you to choose the conclusion that can be drawn from the passage.

Section A sample question and a suggested approach

Multiple choice questions can be on any topic and are very varied. We will use an example to illustrate the points above.

> *Children who live near Sellafield nuclear power station have a higher than average rate of childhood leukaemia. Radiation from the plant is the usual explanation for this higher rate. However, the disease could be caused by a virus. This is because we know that childhood leukaemia is more common in populations with a large influx of newcomers. The population living near Sellafield is a shifting one, with many people coming to work at the plant for a short period, before they are replaced by others. Shifting populations of this type have a higher risk of the virus that leads to leukaemia because of the unusually higher number of contacts within them.*

Which of the following is the best statement of the main conclusion of the above argument?

A   Childhood leukaemia cannot be caused by radiation from nuclear power stations.
B   Shifting populations have a higher risk of childhood leukaemia.
C   The rate of childhood leukaemia is higher than the national average.
D   A virus could be the explanation for the higher rate of childhood leukaemia near Sellafield.

The first sentence gives us a fact about children living near the plant and the second sentence gives us a commonly accepted explanation. So far, there is no argument. We then come across 'however', which is a very significant word in this passage. It signals a change in direction, as what follows is a different explanation for the high rate of childhood leukaemia. As Chapter 7 showed, what follows 'however' is often (but not always) the main conclusion. This is the case here – the main conclusion is that the disease could be caused by a virus.

What follows are the reasons that support this alternative view. Taking the idea that shifting populations have a higher risk of the virus *together with* the idea that Sellafield does have a shifting population gives us reason to believe that the leukaemia at Sellafield may result from a virus.

You should now work through the four answers one by one, thinking of reasons why each one is correct or incorrect:

- The passage shows that there could be two possible explanations for the high rate of leukaemia – radiation and viruses. There is nothing to support the idea that it *cannot* be radiation.
- B gives us a new version of the reasons that support the conclusion. It cannot be the main conclusion if it is a statement of reasons.
- C repeats the fact given to us in the first line.
- D is the correct answer because it is a form of words that suggests that the explanation could be a virus.

Every multiple choice question will be slightly different and it is not possible to approach each one in exactly the same way. In some cases, you may see the correct answer quickly and not need to work through the others. In more complicated examples, you may need to go back to the passage several times to assess a possible answer.

Section B and section C: before you look at the questions

The questions in sections B and C are based on passages included in the exam resource booklet, which you will need to read carefully. The questions will clearly indicate which passage they are based upon. The resource booklet will probably contain one long passage and one or two shorter passages.

It is important that you begin your work on section B by reading the passages carefully. First of all, try and get a general sense of the argument that is presented in the long passage. Ask yourself, what does the author want me to believe? You may find that you need to read the passage a couple of times in order to be clear. After that, go through all the passages and look out for the following:

- indicator words
- any gaps or jumps in the text that might lead to questions about assumptions or flaws
- evidence or examples
- reasons – each paragraph of the longer passage is likely to contain a reason
- conclusions – intermediate or main (overall).

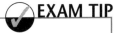
EXAM TIP

Always make sure that you read the passages in the resource booklet very carefully before looking at the questions.

Make your reading active by looking for parts of the argument as you read. Some students find it helpful to underline or highlight particular sections of text.

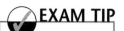

EXAM TIP

The space available for you to write on the exam paper, and the number of marks for each question, can be used as a general guide to how much to write in section B

Section B

The questions in section B are likely to cover the whole range of the OCR specification and will clearly be different from year to year. However, there are certain aspects of the questions that will be the same.

Firstly, you write your answers on the paper. This means that the amount of space given and the marks available tell you quite a lot about how much you should write. Some questions may have only 1 line and 1 mark available. This means that you do not need to write very much to get the mark. Other questions may have 7 or 8 lines and 4 marks available. In this case, you will need to write at more length in order to access all the marks available. Every paper is likely to contain questions that refer to the structure of the argument presented in the long passage. The questions might be of the following style:

> a. Identify the main conclusion of the passage.
>
> b. Identify the intermediate conclusion of the passage.
>
> c. Identify a number of reasons in the passage. (You may be asked to give around five or six.)

There will also be questions asking about assumptions, strengths, weaknesses and flaws in the arguments presented in the passages. The questions might be of the following style:

EXAM TIP

Questions about assumptions are likely to ask you to find assumptions, rather than to evaluate the assumption.

Questions about strengths and weaknesses in the arguments are likely to refer to examples and evidence.

> a. What assumption must be made to support a particular section of reasoning?
>
> b. What is the strength/weakness in the way the author uses a particular example or piece of evidence?
>
> c. Name a flaw in a particular paragraph.
>
> d. Explain the flaw in a particular paragraph.

REMEMBER

The word 'flaw' refers to a specific weakness referred to in the OCR specification and glossary. Flaws need to be identified by their correct label, such as 'slippery slope', 'appeal to popularity' etc. It's also important to explain the flaw.

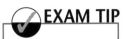

Finally, you should expect questions on other common areas of critical thinking such as analogies, counter arguments and general principles.

Section C

This section will require you to formulate your own arguments in response to the arguments presented in the longer passage in the resource booklet. There may be short answer questions that require you to think of reasons or principles that would be part of a larger argument and questions that ask you to write complete, longer arguments. It may be that you will be asked to write several further arguments, focussed on different parts of the passage. Make sure that you have read the questions carefully so that you know what to write about.

The questions asking for longer arguments are likely to be of the following style:

> *Write a further argument that supports **or** challenges the conclusion of the passage.*

To answer this type of question, you will need all the skills that you practised in Chapter 7. However, first of all you must decide whether to support or challenge the conclusion. See what comes to mind – if you think of several new reasons to support the original conclusion, write your argument accordingly, and vice versa.

The most important exam skill is to recognise that you need to write a *new* argument. You will not receive credit for repeating what is already in the long passage. You can use information or evidence from the passage, but you must put it into a new argument.

Section B and section C sample questions

Section B
Read the following passage and answer all the questions that follow it.

Education begins at home

Teaching children at home has many advantages over sending them to school. We should therefore encourage more parents to teach their children at home.

1

It is in the child's best interests to learn and grow within its family unit. Experts in child development suggest that a child learns most of what is required for human communication between the age of 1 and 5 and when the child is in the constant company of its mother. If the family unit does such a good job before school age, it is obvious that it will continue to do a good job later on. Further support comes from psychologists, who have suggested that our social development also depends upon a stable family unit.

2

Newspaper headlines often feature children who have taken A levels at very early ages and it is not surprising to find that most of these children have been educated at home. In one case, a child taught at home took Maths A level at nine years old. Children working at home are able to develop a greater depth of knowledge, interacting with adults and parents in a way that allows them to learn at their own speed. Home education is the best way to produce gifted and talented children.

3

Many children struggle to attain basic literacy levels and are identified as having special learning needs during their school life. The result? Four out of ten adults in some areas of the country cannot read or write properly and are unable to do simple sums. Fortunately, such perceived problems disappear when children are removed from school, allowed to learn at a slower pace and given one-to-one support from their parents. This shows that home education can solve the problem of learning difficulties.

4

Sadly, state schools fail our children – their learning is restricted by bullying, the narrow demands of the national curriculum and inexperienced, poorly qualified teachers. Worse, the large size of most classes means that students cannot hope to receive any individual attention from their teacher. Expecting teachers to successfully teach such large groups would be like asking doctors to diagnose the illnesses of 30 different patients in a group all at once! Seeing patients individually is what we expect from our doctors; education should be no different.

5

Anyone can teach their children at home – no special skills or qualifications are needed – leading to greater diversity. It has been suggested that home teaching will inevitably lead to a lowering of educational standards. However, teachers learn little on teacher training courses. The exclusive focus is classroom management because so many schools have disruptive pupils. The recent example of a school that had to expel three of its pupils for attacking a teacher proves the point.

6

Finally, home education is very popular. It is estimated that there are now over 50,000 and perhaps as many as 150,000 children taught at home by their parents in the UK. These figures are even more surprising given that parents who educate their children at home do not receive any financial assistance.

7

1. Identify the main conclusion of the argument presented in the passage.

2. Identify two reasons that are given to support the main conclusion.

3. Identify a counter assertion given in the passage.

4. In paragraph 2, the author argues that the family will continue to do a 'good job' because it does a good job for children from the ages of one to five. Name and explain the flaw in the author's reasoning.

5a. What evidence does the author use to support the argument in paragraph 3?

5b. Suggest why this evidence may not support the author's argument in paragraph 3.

6. What must the author assume about the adults who cannot read or write properly in order to support the argument in paragraph 4?

7. In paragraph 5, the author makes use of an analogy. Give one relevant similarity and one relevant dissimilarity in this analogy.

8. Give one weakness in the author's use of the example of the school that expelled three of its pupils in paragraph 6.

Section C

9. Identify a general principle used by the author.

10. Give one reason why it might not be a good idea for a child to complete an A level at age nine.

11. Explain why the evidence given in paragraph 7 does not support the author's argument in paragraph 1.

12. Construct **one** further argument that **challenges or supports** the main conclusion of 'Education begins at home'.

Section B and section C sample answers and examiner's commentary

1. Identify the main conclusion of the argument presented in the passage.

Student A: We should encourage more parents to teach their children at home.
Examiner's comment: A strong answer that uses the exact wording of the passage.

Student B: It would be better if more parents taught their children at home.
Examiner's comment: Although the meaning is similar, it is a stronger statement than that made by the author and is not the correct answer.

2. Identify two reasons that are given to support the main conclusion.

Student A: The child's interests are served by learning in the family. (paragraph 2)
Examiner's comment: This has the basic meaning of the correct answer, but not the accuracy of the original text. The answer would be improved by adding 'best interests' and 'learn and grow' to make it more accurate.

Student B: It is best if the child learns in the family because child development experts support this view. (paragraph 2)
Examiner's comment: This answer makes reference to the evidence provided by the child development experts, which is not part of the reason. This needs to be missed out and more attention paid to the exact wording of the text.

Home education can solve the problem of learning difficulties. (paragraph 3)
Examiner's comment: Exactly as in the text and a perfect answer. Remember that you do not need to agree with the text, only to report what the text suggests.

Home education is better because it does not produce so many illiterate adults. (paragraph 3)
Examiner's comment: This is a very poor answer that has none of the correct meaning. It seems to be a summary of the paragraph, which is unlikely to receive credit in the exam.

3. Identify a counter assertion given in the passage.

Student A: Home teaching will inevitably lead to a lowering of education standards.
Examiner's comment: A strong answer that reflects the wording used by the author.

Student B: Home teaching will lead to lower standards.
Examiner's comment: Certainly worth credit, but by missing out 'inevitably' it changes the emphasis intended by the author.

4. In paragraph 2, the author argues that the family will continue to do a 'good job' because it does a good job for children from the ages of one to five. Name and explain the flaw in the author's reasoning.

Student A: The author uses an 'appeal to history'. This is flawed because the fact that something was successful in the past does not guarantee that it will continue to be successful in the future. This is particularly so in this case because there will be so many differences in a child between one and five and later in childhood.

Examiner's comment: The student has identified the correct term and given an accurate explanation. The answer is helped by reference to the difference in children at different ages to illustrate why what has been successful in the past may not be successful in the future.

Student B: The author makes a 'hasty generalisation'. They assume that it will be successful in the future because it was in the early years of the child's life.

Examiner's comment: This candidate has understood the problem, but not expressed it clearly. The author tells us what s/he thinks will happen, rather than making an assumption, so the answer would be improved by removing this reference. It is often helpful to give an example of why something may not be true in the future.

5a. What evidence does the author use to support the argument in paragraph 3?

Student A: Many of the children reported as taking A levels early have been educated at home.

Examiner's comment: A very strong answer that includes all the information in a succinct way.

Student B: The case of a 9 year old taking Maths A level.

Examiner's comment: This is only the example given by the author. The answer misses the point that the author is suggesting that there are many cases. It would be improved by stating that this person had been educated at home.

5b. Suggest why this evidence may not support the author's argument in paragraph 3.

Student A: It may be that the children were educated at home because they were so clever rather than home education creating the gifted children – the author may have the causal connection the wrong way around.

Examiner's comment: A good answer, but one that does not really address the problem of the evidence used by the author. By making a point about the direction of a causal relationship, this candidate has clearly thought carefully about what is going on. However, there are more straightforward answers.

Student B: It is unlikely that the few children mentioned in the press will be representative of all the children educated at home – it may be that most of the children educated at home are very unsuccessful.

Examiner's comment: A more straightforward approach, but perfectly correct. The author's evidence is very selective and this candidate has clearly understood that.

6. What must the author assume about the adults who cannot read or write properly in order to support the argument in paragraph 4?

Student A: The author needs to assume that the vast majority of the illiterate adults were not educated at home.

Examiner's comment: A strong answer that uses the term 'majority'. In situations like this it is very rare to have to assume that every single example fits the argument.

Student B: The author needs to assume that every one of the adults unable to read and write properly was educated at a school and that the others were educated at home.

Examiner's comment: The candidate seems to have understood what is going on, but has overdone the assumption. It is not necessary to assume that every one of the adults unable to read properly was educated at school – the argument still holds as long as most of the adults unable to read and write came from schools.

7. In paragraph 5, the author makes use of an analogy. Give one relevant similarity and one relevant dissimilarity in this analogy.

Student A: The two situations may be similar in that in both cases there is quite a range of individuals in a group. The 30 patients are unlikely to all have the same illness, just as a class of 30 pupils are unlikely to have the same learning needs or ability.

The analogy does not hold because teaching is a long-term process that takes place over many months and years. We do not judge its success on one moment in time. Doctors on the other hand do need to make a very quick judgement. The two situations are dissimilar in a very important way and the author cannot argue from one to the other.

Examiner's comment: A strong answer as it describes the similarity and dissimilarity that are relevant to the author's argument.

Student B: The two situations are similar because doctors and teachers are both trying to help other people.

They are different in that in one case teachers are trying to give something to pupils that they do not already have – knowledge and learning – whereas doctors are trying to find something that is already there.

Examiner's comment: The first part is very weak. It is true but does not address the relevant part of the analogy to the argument – the idea that the processes of teaching and diagnosing illnesses are similar enough to mean that teaching should only take place individually because doctors only work individually. The second point is better, but is not well explained.

8. Give one weakness in the author's use of the example of the school that expelled three of its pupils in paragraph 6.

Student A: The author cannot use evidence from only one school to make such a strong conclusion about the content of teacher training courses. The evidence may be a very extreme case, whereas teacher training courses are more likely to reflect the general conditions that will be found by teachers.

Examiner's comment: The point illustrates how the author uses evidence that does not support the very strong conclusion that teacher training has an *exclusive* focus on classroom management. We would expect there to be some focus on this issue among all the other topics covered by trainee teachers. It is a very strong answer because it looks at the weak link between the example and the author's point about teacher training courses.

Student B: The author is wrong to generalise from one school to all the others.

Examiner's comment: The answer does not make it clear what is being generalised. An improved version would include that it is not possible to generalise from such extreme behaviour to all schools or that this particular example may not be representative of all schools. It is a weak answer because the link to the nature of teacher training courses is not made.

9. Identify a general principle used by the author.

Student A: Diversity in education is a good thing.

Examiner's comment: The author's whole argument rests to some extent on the idea that an individual timetable of learning is the best for children, or at least a better way than conventional schooling. (Of course, many would argue that children should be reaching the same standard at the same age.) The candidate has nearly captured the point.

Student B: Taking an A level at age 9 is a good thing.

Examiner's comment: This is not really a general principle because it refers to one case rather than all cases. We could improve it by saying that taking A levels early is a good thing so that it includes all the cases mentioned in the press.

10. Give one reason why it might not be a good idea for a child to complete an A level at age nine.

Student A: It might not be a good idea because they will not benefit from the social aspects of university if they go at the age of 10.

Examiner's comment: The candidate thinks of a clear disadvantage in terms of what happens next, and clearly a 10-year-old will not be able to fully participate in all the activities at university.

Student B: They may regret missing out on their childhood.

Examiner's comment: This answer rests on the idea that A levels have stopped the child doing the other things that
9-year-olds typically do. This may or may not be true, and we cannot tell from the information that we are given. A better answer would be to suggest that the time that must have been put into the A level work *may* have stopped them enjoying *all* of the activities enjoyed by 9-year-olds – a more defendable position.

11. **Explain why the evidence given in paragraph 7 does not support the author's argument in paragraph 1.**

> **Student A:** In paragraph 1 the author suggests that home education has many advantages over school. Whether or not something is popular does not affect how good it is and so the information in paragraph 7 does not support the point in paragraph 1. The author is trying to suggest that something is good just because a lot of people do it.
>
> **Examiner's comment:** A strong answer that is accurate and detailed.

> **Student B:** The final paragraph is just figures and does not mention any advantage of teaching children at home.
>
> **Examiner's comment:** Very nearly there and this candidate can see the problem. It would be improved by stating that the reasoning in paragraph 1 is about the advantages of teaching children at home and that paragraph 7 is just about the numbers who do teach children at home.

12. **Construct one further argument that challenges or supports the main conclusion of 'Education begins at home'.**

> **Student A:** Interactions with friends at school help children develop social skills. Working with several teachers helps children to learn to respond positively to different authority figures. For example, children learn to recognise the different authority of teachers, year heads and head teachers.
>
> Therefore, going to school gives children valuable life skills.
>
> In addition, schools are likely to have far better resources, for instance scientific and gym equipment, which will enhance children's learning.
>
> Therefore, we should not encourage more parents to teach their children at home.
>
> **Examiner's comment:** There is a clearly stated main conclusion and a clearly stated intermediate conclusion – going to school gives children valuable life skills. The argument also makes use of the examples of different grades of teacher and examples of equipment that are unlikely to be found at home. A very good attempt at a structured argument.

Student B: Children like going to school as they get to spend time with their friends. Spending all day with adults could mean that children do not enjoy themselves. And anyway, no parent can possibly know as much as all the teachers in a school. Therefore, we should not encourage more parents to teach their children at home.

Examiner's comment: This candidate has a clearly stated conclusion and several reasons that support it to some extent. However, the first sentence will only support the conclusion if we show that spending time with friends has some benefit, such as improving social skills. We could improve the third sentence by suggesting that no parent could have all the skills, experience and resources available in a school, as teaching is about more than just knowing something. Overall it is not a strong argument because the reasons only offer limited support to the conclusion and there is no intermediate conclusion. There are no examples or evidence used to support the points made.

Guidance to the activities

ACTIVITY ❶

a) (**reason**) The sun is very strong today and (**reason**) you are going to lie on the beach. (**conclusion**) You should put plenty of sun cream on.

b) (**reason**) Heavy snow is predicted later on. (**reason**) The police are advising everyone to stay at home. (**conclusion**) You should not leave home to go to work.

c) (**reason**) You are allergic to dog hair. (**reason**) The friends you are going to visit have a dog. (**conclusion**) You should take some medication to reduce your allergic reaction.

ACTIVITY ❸

Passage a) is an **account**. There is a description of what happened without any attempt to persuade us of any particular point.

Passage b) is an **opinion**. It seems as if there is an argument here, but there is no conclusion. The conclusion might be something like 'We should go to Brighton on a different day.' You might see this passage as several reasons without a conclusion. It only becomes an argument when we add the conclusion.

Passage c) is an **argument**. The passage contains a number of reasons that lead to the conclusion that I should book a holiday at a seaside resort.

Passage d) is an **opinion**. The comment shows us that the author has a strong view on the topic, but s/he gives us no reasons why we should share this view.

ACTIVITY ❹

Passage a) is an **explanation**. The non-arrival of the train would not be open to dispute. The explanation for it not arriving is given as a fallen tree.

Passage b) is an **argument**. The passage is trying to persuade you that you should catch an earlier bus than usual (the conclusion). The reasons are that the traffic is unusually heavy today and that it is very important that you get to school on time.

Passage c) is an **explanation**. The increase in GCSE results is a widely accepted statistic. The explanation is that this is caused by better teaching and by improved funding for schools.

Passage d) is a slightly longer **argument**. It seeks to persuade a family with small children that wants a pet to get a dog. What follows the conclusion are the reasons for believing this point.

ACTIVITY

a) (**therefore**) Trains are a better way to travel than a car. (**because**) It is possible to read during the journey and (**because**) there is no need to worry about traffic jams or breakdowns.

b) (**therefore**) Football is not as exciting as commentators suggest. (**because**) Many games end 0-0 and (**because**) results only matter for teams at the top or bottom of a table.

ACTIVITY 6

a) R1   Gas is an inexpensive way to heat your home.
   R2   Gas heating boilers are small and neat.
   C   You should install gas central heating to heat your home.

The two reasons are acting independently.

b) R1   Spending a long time in front of a computer screen can cause eye strain.
   R2   You've been working on your homework on the computer for several hours.
   C   You should have a break from the computer.

The two reasons are acting jointly.

c) R1   Hair dye can ruin the condition of your hair.
   R2   You have had your hair dyed several times recently.
   C   You would be wise to use conditioner to improve the condition of your hair.

The two reasons are acting jointly.

ACTIVITY

a) R1   Coffee contains caffeine, which is a stimulant.
   R2   Taking any stimulant before going to bed stops you from sleeping soundly
   IC   so drinking coffee before going to bed will stop you from sleeping soundly.
   R3   A poor night's sleep may lead you to feel tired in the morning.
   C   Therefore drinking coffee before going to bed may cause you to feel tired in the morning.

b) Heather and Bill have been living together happily for five years. [= just an introduction to the argument]
- R1 They plan to keep their relationship healthy by taking up new activities and interests
- R2 as well as setting aside time to discuss their relationship.
- IC They have in place good strategies to help them in the future.
- R3 Many experts suggest that happy relationships rely on just these type of strategies.
- C It is therefore likely that Heather and Bill will continue to live together happily.

c)
- R1 To keep healthy you are advised to have five portions of fresh fruit or vegetables each day.
- R2 You have only had four so far today
- IC so you should have a piece of fruit.
- R3 We only have apples and oranges
- R4 and you do not like oranges
- C so you should have an apple to maintain your good health.

ACTIVITY 9

a) The author must assume several things: that cost and/or size are the most important factors in choosing a central heating system; that it is possible to have gas central heating (i.e. that there is a connection to the gas main); that the home needs central heating.

b) The author must assume two things – that a car is the only way that Raj is able to transport his drum kit to gigs and that a guitar does not need car transport to get to gigs.

c) The author needs to assume that the normal bus will not arrive on time in the current traffic conditions'; also that the earlier bus is early enough to allow for the increased traffic and will arrive on time.

Arguments can contain several assumptions. The answers above are some of the important ones. If you think that you have found another, don't automatically think that you must be wrong (or right), but check with your teacher.

ACTIVITY 10

a) The correct answer is C. The author's main point is that money should be injected into the situation to prevent the brain drain. For this to solve the problem we must assume that it was a financial reason that led to the brain drain in the first place. This assumption is what C expresses

The author does not need to assume A. The argument is that some scientists have gone abroad, but there is no implication that all of them have. It is not in the passage; but it is not an assumption. We also do not need B for the argument to stand. The author is arguing about stopping the brain drain, not bringing scientists back. It is not in the passage, but would be part of a different argument, that is about how we bring scientists back. D may or may not be true, but given that the author is arguing about scientists, it really does not matter for the argument if other professionals were attracted abroad. Therefore we do not need to assume that it is only scientists who were attracted abroad.

ACTIVITY ⓫

Here are some possible answers:

a) The author needs to assume that in a significant percentage [or a significant proportion] of cases the act of giving up smoking will lead to the ex-smoker having no smoking-related illnesses that put a strain on the health service. [This is, of course, unlikely since smoking-related diseases may still appear years later after stopping smoking. Although it is not a very likely occurrence, the author's argument does not work without it.]

b) The author needs to assume that most children [but definitely not all children] have access to a library with a specialist adviser.

c) The author needs to assume that rules and tactics are the only aspects of rugby or football that make it exciting.

ACTIVITY ⓬

R1   We cannot dispute that we need vitamins.

R2   It seems that fruit and vegetables have real benefits over vitamin tablets.

R3   We don't need to damage our wealth by buying pills to protect our health.

R4   Mega doses of vitamins can have toxic effects.

C   Taking vitamins and food supplements is neither good nor bad but unnecessary for most of us.

ACTIVITY 13

a) E1   Researchers combined hospital admission numbers with sport participation figures across the US in the 1990s. For every 10,000 participants, they found overall neck injuries in 5.85 football players.

E2   That's more than the 2.8 hockey players and 1.67 soccer players combined.

R   American football is the sport most likely to cause neck injury in the US.

C   Students concerned for their long term health should avoid American football.

ACTIVITY 14

a) F1   drivers must surely count amongst the elite of multi-taskers.

b) R1   Driving skill is an essential quality in an F1 driver.

R2   F1 drivers have to be among the very fittest athletes in the world.

R3   They need to be competent engineers as well.

R4   The right mental approach is critical.

R5   Drivers have to perform all these amazing feats at the same time, at 200 mph.

c) Evidence in Paragraph 1: Recent rule changes have reduced downforce, required drivers to use the same tyres for the whole race, and keep the same engine for two race meetings.

Evidence in Paragraph 2: A typical F1 race can last an hour and a half.

The example about Jensen Button includes the following evidence: neck muscles support a weight equivalent to 30 bags of sugar. Pulling 3.5 G through the 150 mph bend.

No evidence in paragraphs 3 or 4.

d) The example of Jensen Button is used in paragraph 2 to illustrate the forces exerted on a particular driver, and Martin Brundle's actions following a major accident are used in paragraph 4 to illustrate the mental attitude needed by drivers.

ACTIVITY 15

R1   Learning a musical instrument encourages children to concentrate.

R2   Learning music improves mathematical ability.

R3   Music is the poetry of the soul.

R4   Being able to play an instrument is socially useful.

IC   Music clearly has many benefits.

C   Therefore all children should have the opportunity to learn an instrument.

ACTIVITY 16

The conclusion is, 'We should embrace the many advantages offered by the health and beauty industry.'

'Yoga is nothing to a good manicure' contradicts 'Exercise is the best way to improve the way you feel about yourself.'

There are many inconsistencies:

- 'Yoga is nothing to a good manicure' is inconsistent with 'Knowing that your muscle tone is just right', as yoga would be a much better way of getting your muscle tone just right than a manicure.

- 'You cannot achieve inner serenity if your hair, nails and skin are not perfect' is inconsistent with 'Image is not everything.'

- It is inconsistent to reject the exercise offered by walking or cycling if exercise is 'the best way to improve the way you feel about yourself'. It is particularly inconsistent, since working out in the gym is not known for its sweet-smelling results.

- It is inconsistent to say that gym membership can cost £120 a month, but that 'it doesn't make sense to reject the many facilities offered'. Almost all these facilities can be acquired for much less money.

- Deep acceptance of ourselves is inconsistent with the emphasis on superficial looks throughout the passage, particularly in the second paragraph.

'Some people may prefer to walk their dogs or cycle, but …' is an example of a counter argument.

ACTIVITY 17

Paragraphs 1 and 4 assume that flying is the only means of international travel.

Paragraph 1 assumes that carbon dioxide has a fatal effect on the planet and that emissions from aircraft are sufficient to kill the world.

Paragraph 2 assumes that uncontrolled and uncontrollable are the same.

Paragraph 3 assumes that travel is mainly (entirely?) for business purposes.

ACTIVITY 18

a) I should walk the dog first (before it rains).

b) Girls care more about clothing than boys. Boys are more interested in hobbies than girls. All children spend a large amount of money every week.

c) The population is ageing.

d) 2

e) 3

ACTIVITY 19

a) The number of people in prison has risen by 20% since when? Has the general population also risen by 20% in the same time period? Has crime really risen or have the police become better at catching criminals? There is no timescale for this rise. It's possible that the population has risen by the some amount. We cannot be sure that crime has risen; the police may have become better at catching criminals or the judicial system more likely to imprison offenders.

b) Here the evidence is from Russia, and compares the cost of home grown vegetables with prices in markets. The evidence cannot, therefore, be used to support a conclusion about the relative prices of vegetables in British supermarkets and those grown at home. It is also undated, so we do not know if this evidence is from 2005 or 1805.

ACTIVITY 20

a) We have to ask how representative of Americans people in Texas are. They have a different culture and world view from people on the East Coast, for example. Texas is also the home of George Bush. This poll excludes most working people, people who stay at home, people who have the sense to avoid anyone approaching them with a clipboard... It does not give us a clear guide as to what Americans think. It tells us what Texans who have time and money to shop during working hours think.

b) This applies a valid statistic for the whole population to too small a group. The people we know are generally speaking, unrepresentative of the population as a whole.

c) Who was asked? People who visit National Trust properties or visit their website? Older people who remember the white cliffs as the first view of home after a trip abroad (rather than the local airport), possibly even returning from the war? People who live in Kent? Can we really say that 22% counts as a runaway winner? Would it have been more accurate to say that votes were split?

ACTIVITY 21

Because not everybody is average, some people will earn well under average wages. Some of these may also spend considerably over average on the lottery. This would mean that a particular family may be spending a much greater than average percentage of their income on lottery tickets, perhaps instead of buying more nutritious food.

ACTIVITY 22

a) Silk is a weak example because it is not typical of natural fibres – it is particularly easy to ruin. Cotton, a natural fibre in common use, is easier to care for than many man-made fibres. Neoprene is a good example of a man-made fibre which allows unusual activities. However, this is not really an example of adapting to weather conditions: it is more an example of refusing to adapt. Reindeer fur and fat are apparently better than man-made fibres for adapting to cold weather.

b) This is an extreme example. Although a marathon runner may be able to get from the suburbs to central London faster than Clarkson in a car, most of us would not be able to. A better example would be of a normal person walking a mile faster than a car can be driven.

ACTIVITY 23

Main conclusion

If a man wants to impress a woman, he needs to let her know with his opening gambit that he is cultured, generous and physically fit, but not boastful.

Psychologists' data

It is difficult to separate the effectiveness of a chat up line from the other characteristics of the speaker and listener. Who tested the lines? How attractive were they? Neither academic psychologists nor undergraduates would be representative of the typical male. How typical are the 'verbal signals of genetic quality' arrived at by a group of academics?

How attractive, intelligent and cultured were the women? Under what circumstances did the testing take place – in a bar, or in a lab? Did women rank chat up lines on a computer screen? Were all 40 chat up lines tried on the women one after the other? Or were they tried one at a time? Both approaches are problematic.

The study begs the question (see Chapter 5). The psychologists have started from the principle that men should be demonstrating their quality to passive women who accept or decline an offer. They have devised chat up lines which reflect this theory and then taken the most successful of their sample to be actually successful, without comparing it with other approaches.

The study, as reported here, is not big enough, nor well enough designed, to produce statistically meaningful evidence. It would require an enormous survey to iron out the effects of cultural and individual preferences.

The Independent on Sunday test

This test should be treated as an example rather than as evidence – one reporter in one bar, in central London, which is in any case not representative of the rest of the country. One unflattering response does not disprove a theory that a particular chat up line might be effective in general. However, as an example of the kind of responses which might be gained, it is an amusing way of undermining the study.

ACTIVITY 24

a) Appeal to history – just because the train has not been late before does not mean it will not be late tonight.

b) Appeal to authority. The National Lottery organiser is a poor authority because it is likely to be biased.

c) Appeal to popularity. However, governments sometimes have to do unpopular things, even in a democracy.

ACTIVITY 25

a) A is correct. It expresses an appeal to tradition. However, traditional is not the same as right.

B is incorrect, as we have not been told that smoking in public is popular.

C is incorrect, as the argument is not suggesting what we might do in the future.

D is incorrect – it simply disagrees with the argument.

b) C is correct. It expresses the flaw that popularity is not enough to justify a conclusion.

A is incorrect, as the fact that everyone loves something is no better a reason to hate something than to love it.

B simply re-states the argument.

D does not express a flaw.

ACTIVITY 26

a) Tu quoque argument. We cannot justify a wrong action on the basis that the French are also doing it.

b) Generalisation. We cannot conclude that genetically modified crops (in general) are too dangerous for human consumption on the basis of one crop.

c) Tu quoque argument. If it is wrong to exploit illegal immigrants, the fact that other companies do it does not make it right for us.

ACTIVITY 27

a) D is correct, as it expresses a sweeping generalisation.

A expresses a hasty generalisation. It would be a flaw, but it is not the pattern of reasoning in this text.

B would express a sweeping generalisation, but it refers to the common prejudice that women are poor drivers. The text, however, suggests that Susan Lovegood was a good driver because she was a woman.

C is too vague an answer to be useful!

b) B is correct, as one wrong action cannot justify another.

A is an assumption of the argument. We might wish to challenge it, but it is not a flaw in the pattern of reasoning.

C is not a flaw in the argument. It is, perhaps, an extreme extension of the argument, but it is wide of the mark. The argument aims at the hypocrisy of people who treat animals badly criticising others for keeping animals badly.

D is incorrect as the argument is not generalising from chickens to dogs.

ACTIVITY 28

a) Restricting the options. It may be possible to ensure the survival of wolves in captivity.

b) Restricting the options – there may be another solution than going to Lapland. Slippery slope – unlinked extreme sequences of events.

c) Flaw of causation. It is not the weather reporters who cause the weather. Their understanding of what the weather will do causes the reports.

ACTIVITY 29

a) D is correct, as it expresses a flaw of causation. There may be other causes for the public's perception, such as concern for wildlife.

A is incorrect. The argument is not flawed because it is unfair, but because it assumes a causal link which may not exist.

B tries to make you think that the flaw is restricting the options. But the new crops may benefit farmers as well as consumers.

C tries to make you think that the flaw is a slippery slope, but it is not. The soya bean is one example of a crop which might directly influence public opinion.

b) B is correct, as it expresses the flaw of restricting the options. There may be other ways of expressing your true personality.

A would suggest that you are mistaken, which is different from using a flawed pattern of reasoning.

C aims to make you think that the argument is a slippery slope.

D suggests that there is a flaw of causation in the argument.

ACTIVITY 30

a) Attacking the arguer – dismissing scientists' arguments because of who they are rather than examining the arguments. It also restricts the options – either you're a scientist or you value the important things in life.

b) This begs the question.

c) This confuses a necessary condition with sufficient one. Qualifications and experience may be necessary to get the job, but they are not enough – there may be questions of personality, preparation, interview technique or even better qualified candidates.

ACTIVITY 31

a) A is correct. Although beauty may be necessary for success in cosmetics, it is not sufficient. This make up may be too expensive, too difficult to make in sufficient quantities or simply not catch on.

B reverses the confusion of necessary and sufficient conditions so that it does not apply.

C aims to make you think that there is a flaw of causation. However, it does not matter for this argument why people use make up, so long as enough people are attracted by the beauty of the cosmetic in question.

D may express a correct observation, but this is not a flaw in the argument.

b) B is correct, as it expresses the flaw of attacking the arguer rather than the argument. Mathilda Plume's vested interest does not guarantee that her claims are wrong.

A is incorrect. Mathilda Plume does not generalise, nor does she suggest that smoking is safe.

C suggests incorrectly that there is a straw person flaw.

D is incorrect. The argument uses the attack on Plume to suggest that we can accept figures about smoking deaths. However, it is Plume who suggests that they are distorted.

ACTIVITY 32

a) C is correct.

b) The argument uses justice as meaning 'ensuring that an offender is punished'. It is almost synonymous with revenge in this argument, so it goes further than the answer. This use of justice ignores the idea of fairness or impartiality towards an offender and assumes that a victim has a greater right to see someone punished than an accused person has to be treated fairly. It assumes that people not convicted were guilty, and/or that it is legal incompetence which has led to lack of conviction rather than innocence.

ACTIVITY 33

University staff is conflated with pen-pushers.

ACTIVITY 34

a) Principle

b) Opinion

c) Hypothetical claim

d) Fact

e) Probably opinion. It may be factual if it can be verified. There is a fine line.

ACTIVITY 36

a) We should put the future of the world before our selfish desires.

b) We should not hurt animals.

c) It is not fair that genuinely ill people have to wait for treatment.

ACTIVITY 37

a) This is a comparison between different ways of understanding numbers. We are simply meant to gain a clearer picture of the numbers dying. There is no question of complete parallels involving agency of pilot, blame etc.

b) This is an analogy between certain kinds of criminal and cancer.

c) This is a comparison. The only similarity required is logical organisation. We do not need to accept, for example, that her mind has no processing power and is merely a storage unit.

ACTIVITY 38

a) Comparison: Parallel between darts and reading to support the conclusion that darts should not be an olympic sport.

Similarities: neither darts nor reading involves physical prowess (in the same way as traditional olympic sports such as sprinting, jumping or running a marathon). Both require skill.

Differences: darts requires mainly physical technique, whereas reading is mainly a mental exercise. Darts has clear rules and a strong, existing competitive thread. Reading is a solitary activity which does not lend itself easily to competition. Darts makes interesting spectator viewing, whereas watching someone read is dull.

Overall, although the analogy helps the reader to consider what is required for an olympic sport, the differences are significant. It lends little support to the conclusion because, on close examination, darts actually seems to fit the criteria for sport (at least in comparison with reading).

b) Comparison: a parallel between the relationships between intelligent design (ID)/evolution and astrology/astronomy.

Similarities:

o This analogy clearly shows intelligent design and evolution to be in the same relationship as astrology, which scientists consider as vague and woolly at best, and astronomy, which is a well-regarded science.

o People may believe in astrology, but their belief is not supported by scientific evidence, and even astrologers would not claim that their art should be taught in science classes. Intelligent design is similarly based on belief rather than evidence.

Differences: One important difference between the relationships is that astrology and astronomy are using the stars for different purposes. Astrologers seek meaning in the stars which applies to human life, whereas astronomers attempt to understand the physics of space. Intelligent design and evolution, however, are both trying to do the same thing – explain the origins of man. ID suggests that we were designed, whereas evolution suggests that we are the product of chance. Thus ID and evolution are in direct conflict in their aims in a way that astrology and astronomy are not.

This difference is probably not enough to seriously weaken the analogy because the conclusion was that there is no scientific controversy between ID and evolution. Our evaluation of the analogy allows that there is controversy, but that it is conflict between religion and science rather than between two scientific theories.

c) Comparison: analogy between researching GM crops and setting off a nuclear bomb.

Similarities: both involve allowing bad consequences to come about in order to see how bad they are.

Differences: scale.

Overall, weak because of exaggeration.

ACTIVITY 40

Principle: 'In order to aid poorer nations, we must focus on developing their own skills base.' It is general in so far as it applies to more than one situation. This principle acts as the conclusion, supported by reasoning.

Hypothetical claim: 'If Africa had its own science and technology base, this balance would be redressed.' This seems a likely consequence. However, interventions to help

Africa acquire a technology base may be a drop in the ocean. Redressing such an uneven balance is a major task. One alternative consequence might be that educated Africans are better placed to migrate.

Hypothetical reasoning: 'If Africa can develop centres of excellence in science and technology, it will be able to close the scientific gap with the rest of the world.' The consequence here is probably too strongly worded. Africa may be able to narrow the gap, but closing it will probably take more than centres of excellence. A good starting point is being conflated with achieving a desired end.

'It will be able to provide a skills base right across the educational system.' There is quite a leap here, because funding, government support and some cultural change will also be necessary. This can be led by centres of excellence, but such centres alone are unlikely to radically alter the whole educational system.

'From this will come the capacity to provide, for example, clean water and hygienic living conditions.' If centres of excellence can improve skills generally, this will give Africans the ability to improve their living conditions. Overall, centres of scientific excellence are a good idea, and are likely to lead to improvements, but the argument makes claims which are too strong.

Analogy: We do not encourage mature, independent adults by continuing to spoon feed them beyond babyhood. Neither will we encourage the poorest countries in the world to develop to maturity unless we allow them access to the spoon.

The analogy compares the relationship between poorest countries and richest to the adult–child relationship. It specifically says the way forward is like helping a child to achieve independence.

Similarities: the poorest countries are to a certain extent dependent on the richest. Allowing a child to make mistakes with a spoon will assist the learning and development. Giving poor countries the spoon of science will assist learning and development.

Differences: it assumes the spoon is ours to give. This is unfairly patronising.

Overall, the idea of controlling the spoon is a good analogy, but the rich countries' agency as parents is a poor analogy.

ACTIVITY 41

The following are just examples of possible answers. You may have chosen different reasons.

a) It is my birthday and it is traditional to buy drinks for someone on their birthday.
   [joint support – both are needed to support the conclusion]

b) I have worked lots of extra hours. I have been covering the work of a more senior employee while they are away. [independent support – either supports the conclusion]

c) My phone has all the latest features and is also very stylish. [independent support]

d) There are many opportunities for promotion and there is the chance to make a difference in young people's lives. [independent support]

ACTIVITY 42

Both (a) and (d) are very strong conclusions in that they give us very specific outcomes. (a) suggests that clam shell phones are 'much better'. We could make this one weaker by saying that they have some advantages or that they are better in some situations. (d) suggests that reducing fat in our diet 'prevents' heart disease. We are unlikely to be able to argue for such an outcome, given all the other factors involved in heart disease. A weaker conclusion would be that reducing fat in our diet reduces the risk of heart disease.

(b) and (c) are more general, weaker conclusions.

ACTIVITY 43

Some possible arguments:

a) R   Cats do not need to be taken for walks (unlike dogs).

    R   Cats can be left on their own during the day (unlike dogs).

    IC   Therefore cats are easier to look after.

    R   Most people's busy lives means that they do not have much time to look after their pet.

    C   Therefore, cats are better pets than dogs.

b) R   Fish feel pain from the hook.

    R   Fish suffer when out of the water.

    IC   Fishing results in distress to the fish.

    R   There is no purpose in the activity, as the fish are not eaten once caught.

    C   We should consider banning the sport of fishing.

c) R   Traffic speeds are far higher on motorways than on normal roads.

    R   Motorways have three lanes of traffic, unlike all other types of road.

    IC   There are significant differences between motorways and other roads.

    R   Newly qualified drivers only have experience of these other types of road.

    C   Therefore newly qualified drivers should not be allowed to drive on motorways.

All of the above arguments could be improved by including unstated assumptions as an extra reason.

ACTIVITY 44

Two possible answers, for arguments (a) and (c):

a) R   Cats do not need to be taken for walks (unlike dogs).

    Ev   Cats get exercise catching mice and chasing each other.

    R   Cats can be left on their own during the day (unlike dogs).

    Ev   Dogs often destroy furniture if they are bored when left on their own.

    IC   Therefore cats are easier to look after.

    R   Most people's busy lives means that they do not have much time to look after their pet.

    Ex   A working person may only have one or two hours free in the evening.

    C   Therefore, cats are better pets than dogs.

c) R   Traffic speeds are far higher on motorways than on normal roads.

    Ev   The speed limit is 70 mph.

    R   Motorways have three lanes of traffic, unlike all other types of road.

    IC   There are significant differences between motorways and other roads.

    R   Newly qualified drivers only have experience of these other types of road.

    Ex   Such as single carriageway A roads.

    C   Therefore newly qualified drivers should not be allowed to drive on motorways.

ACTIVITY 45

Two possible answers:

a) CA   Although the Olympic games are very expensive,

   R   They are a source of great national pride.

   R   They inspire many new sportsmen and women.

   Ev   The success of British athletes in the past has increased participation in the sports that they were successful in.

   IC   The value of the games should not be measured only in financial terms.

   R   The London bid will also involve the regeneration of a 'brownfield' site that will give local people excellent facilities for years to come.

   C   Therefore it is not to be regretted that London won the 2012 games.

b) CA   Although both acts require a level of responsibility,

   R   Driving requires only a simple understanding of the safety of others.

   R   Voting requires a level of maturity and understanding of complex issues surrounding society

   Ex   Elections involve discussion of tax, crime and foreign policy, all of which are difficult to understand.

   IC   There are significant differences between the level of responsibility of the two acts.

   R   Older teenagers tend to be more mature and responsible than younger teenagers.

   C   The age for driving should remain lower than that for voting.

You could have argued that both should be reduced to 17.

Glossary

Ambiguous – a word is ambiguous if it can have more than one meaning and it is not clear which meaning is intended in a particular context

Analogy – a form of argument which uses parallel situations to encourage the reader to accept a conclusion

Analyse – break an argument down into its component parts

Appeal to authority – claiming your conclusion must be right because an expert or someone in authority supports it. This is a flaw in reasoning

Appeal to history – a form of argument which supports a conclusion by reference to trends or actions from the past. This is a flaw in reasoning

Appeal to popularity – a form of argument which supports a conclusion by reference to the beliefs or views of a large number of people. This is a flaw in reasoning.

Argument indicator – a word or short phrase that helps us identify the parts of an argument. For example, 'because' indicates a reason and 'therefore' indicates a conclusion

Assumption – a missing step or reason in an argument. Assumptions are not stated in the argument, but are needed to make the argument work

Attacking the arguer – attacking the person putting forward an argument rather than their argument. This is a flaw in reasoning, as an argument should be judged on its own merits

Circular argument – an argument that starts and ends with the same point. This is a flaw in reasoning

Claim – something which is stated, or claimed to be the case

Conclusion – a statement of something that you should/shouldn't do or believe on the basis of the reasons given

Conflation – bringing two or more different concepts or ideas together and treating them as if they were similar

Confusing necessary and sufficient conditions – reasoning which confuses necessary and sufficient conditions does not support a conclusion. Something which is necessary is not always enough. Something which is enough is not always necessary

Contradiction – bits of the argument that are saying completely opposite things

Counter argument – an argument that puts forward an opposing line of reasoning. Authors may include a counter argument in order to dismiss it, thus supporting their own argument.

Counter reason or **counter assertion** – a reason that would support an opponent's argument. Authors may include a counter reason in order to show the weaknesses in the opponent's argument.

Evaluate – judge whether an argument is strong or weak

Evidence – something used to support, illustrate or develop a reason. Evidence includes statements of fact, statistical claims, personal observations and statements from sources

Explanation – a reason or reasons given to explain why or how something is the case

Flaw – a fault in the pattern of reasoning which weakens the support given to the conclusion of an argument

Flaw of causation – a flaw in reasoning which assumes that if two things occur together or in quick succession, one of them must cause the other. However, this is not enough to infer a causal link Also known as the 'post hoc' flaw

General principle – a statement which applies to a wide range of situations, rather like a rule. A principle can act as a reason, intermediate conclusion, assumption or conclusion in an argument

Generalisation – drawing a general conclusion from specific evidence. This is a flaw in reasoning

Hypothetical claim – an 'if … then' statement used in hypothetical reasoning

Inconsistency – bits of the argument that don't work together, as they pull in different directions. They don't have to pull in completely opposite directions, although a contradiction is a special kind of inconsistency

Intermediate conclusion – a conclusion that is formed on the way to the main conclusion. The intermediate conclusion acts as a reason for the main conclusion.

Main (or **overall**) **conclusion** – a statement of something that you should/shouldn't do or believe that is supported by reasoning in the passage.

Reason – a statement that aims to persuade you to accept a conclusion

Restricting the options – presenting a false and limited version of the choices available to encourage a particular course of action. This is a flaw in reasoning

Slippery slope – reasoning that is based on the idea that one small change or step will inevitably lead to a dramatic change or a whole series of separate steps. Slippery slopes result in extreme conclusions that are not supported by reasoning. This is a flaw in reasoning.

Straw person – deliberately creating a weakened version of an argument (by giving a distorted or extreme version) in order to be able to dismiss that argument. This is a flaw in reasoning as it does not provide a good reason for not accepting the original argument.

Tu quoque – an attempt to justify an action on the basis that someone else is doing it. Often called 'two wrongs do not make a right' when an attempt is made to justify something harmful on the basis of another, different, harmful thing.

Two wrongs don't make a right – an attempt to justify one harmful thing on the basis of another, different, harmful thing. This is a flaw in reasoning, as one wrong action cannot justify another wrong action

Index